THE
RACE
FOR LIFE

THE RACE FOR LIFE

MEMOIRS OF A RWANDAN GENOCIDE SURVIVOR

THEO MAKOMBE

TATE PUBLISHING
AND ENTERPRISES, LLC

The Race for Life
Copyright © 2014 by Theo Makombe. All rights reserved.

All Scriptures are from the *New International Version* of the Bible, © 1989–1995, Zondervan Corporation.

The opinions expressed by the author are not necessarily those of Tate Publishing, LLC.

Published by Tate Publishing & Enterprises, LLC
127 E. Trade Center Terrace | Mustang, Oklahoma 73064 USA
1.888.361.9473 | www.tatepublishing.com

Tate Publishing is committed to excellence in the publishing industry. The company reflects the philosophy established by the founders, based on Psalm 68:11,
"The Lord gave the word and great was the company of those who published it."

Published in the United States of America

ISBN: 978-1-63122-442-3
1. Biography & Autobiography / Cultural Heritage
2. History / Africa / East
14.04.14

This book is dedicated to the family of Makombe.

In memory of
my father, Andre Makombe,
my mother, Mukaruziga Marie,
my brother, Nsanzimfura Felecien,
my sister, Uwamahoro Christina,
my brother, Rwandekwe Emmanuel

To the slain families of my grandfather, Bihigi, who also lost his life: Mfuruta Joseph, Musirikare, and Anonciate Mukamageza. And all the Biguri family who had been killed over the years. We are your children who are left alive. We will stay united to make your lives valued as an appreciation to you for laying the foundations for our lives. You took care of our past; we will take care of your future.

To the slain families of my grandfather, Joas Karera, who also lost his life, of Mwizerwa Silas, and of Kwizera Samuel and all their children, whom we lost during the 1994 tragedy. We will miss you greatly. May God keep you in his sight happily until that day when we will all join in ceremony. You are not dead in our memories.

To all the Rukumbeli community—those who passed away and those still alive—I encourage you to look after one another for the united stand longer and stronger.

ACKNOWLEDGMENTS

First, I want to express my appreciation to my church family, Hope Community Church in Springfield, Missouri, who encouraged me daily to write this book and offered many prayers that lifted me up in my struggles.

Thank you to Connie McKeen, who motivated me to start again when my hope for this book was running out. You are a true friend who has shown me the love of Jesus.

Thanks to Dennis Everson, who often encouraged me and checked on our progress, showing his true love for us.

Thank you to Deborah Schaulis, who used her editorial talent and passion for the Lord to complete this manuscript in expert fashion. We are blessed to have made a friend in her.

I want to thank Mark Phelps and Casey Alvarez, who also contributed to the finished product.

Thanks to my wife, who spent a lot of time editing this work, often going without sleep. She is my encourager and my hero and was with me every step of the way. Also thanks to my children, who brought me joy when I couldn't feel it.

Thanks also to my YWAM family in Rwanda and Scotland, who helped me feel myself again and gain the confidence to write my story. I can't thank YWAM ministries enough, in general, for transforming lives around the world, including mine.

I want to thank my biological family who survived the genocide and supported and encouraged me to grow and become the man I am today. May God bless all those who helped me understand the call on my life. My life could have been cut short if I hadn't found its purpose.

I want personally to thank the RPF Inkotanyi and leadership, who threw themselves into danger to save many innocent lives, including mine.

CONTENTS

Foreword... 11

Introduction... 15

Chapter 1   My Early Years 19
Chapter 2   Running for Our Lives 31
Chapter 3   Deliverance and Reunions 51
Chapter 4   After the Genocide............................. 63
Chapter 5   Back to School.................................... 77
Chapter 6   Shame... 87
Chapter 7   New Life.. 95
Chapter 8   You Can't Stand on Both Sides........... 111
Chapter 9   Learning to Walk in Integrity and Faith.......... 121
Chapter 10 Intercultural Love Story 133
Chapter 11 A Vision of Hope 153
Chapter 12 A Great Promise.................................. 159
Chapter 13 The Zeal to Reach Out 169
Chapter 14 Sin Development................................. 179
Chapter 15 Spiritual Training................................ 189
Chapter 16 True Repentance and Healing 193

FOREWORD

As you read this book, my hope is that your life will never be the same. I pray your eyes will be opened to the war that is all around us and the immeasurably great power God provides for those who truly believe. The war is great, but our God is far greater.

In 2007, God began opening my eyes to see what He had done in my life, and I was so amazed by His wonders. He told me to write a book about it. I thought it would take only three pages because there were so many stories that I did not think I could tell. I was scared to talk about some things, and my heart was wounded by them.

I had so many excuses. One of them was that I don't know how to write a book. I had never really used a computer before, and now I was supposed to type a whole book. There was no one to help me, and I had no money. I was a missionary in Scotland with Youth with a Mission (YWAM). But God encouraged me to try to do all I could.

Once I sat down and tried to write, all these stories came rushing into my mind like a wind. Then I could not believe one book could be enough to contain them all! As I wrote, I began to remember my past. I would write two pages and run back into my bedroom and cry. I hated to remember, but I had to, because it helped me to heal. Then I decided to go ahead and write everything, while crying and grieving for my loss as I made myself remember all the horrors I experienced when I ran for my life for thirty days. As I told my stories and finally grieved, I was set free from many unwelcome burdens.

I went back home to Rwanda the next year and tried to print my story in my native language. Unfortunately, it wasn't organized well, and I had no one to edit it for me. It was too expensive, so I decided to quit.

In 2008, I flew to America with my family just for a visit. For some reason, we were given permanent visas, and I never thought about why we applied for a green card. Later, I knew God was calling me to be a missionary in America.

The first year we lived in Greenville, Ohio, was very hard. I found it difficult to relate in the cold culture, where you meet people only at church and at work but still don't have time to talk to anyone, even if they live in your neighborhood. Missions was in my blood, but in this place, I felt so useless and unable to do anything. Work was too hard for me because I did not understand why God brought me here to be so quiet and attend church every Sunday with nothing to do there. I tried to talk to people about Jesus, but they looked at me as if I was an idiot.

In 2009, I moved to Missouri from Ohio. I found a church where they loved me and welcomed me. It took another year to understand what God was doing. Different groups invited me to tell them how I survived the genocide in Rwanda. Among these were Christian Business Men's Fellowship, churches, a public school, and various Bible studies and families.

That year I learned that almost every American claims to be a Christian so very few people welcomed my attempts to share the gospel with them. They all said that they were already Christian, insinuating that I did not need to witness to them. But then when I wanted to talk about Jesus with them as a brother in Christ, many said they weren't into the whole church thing or made some other excuse to not have to talk about it. I soon discovered that religion was a taboo subject even among so-called fellow believers. I longed for Christian fellowship and edification in the body of Christ. Few of the "Christians" I encountered even wanted to talk about God.

Their lives were so different from what the Bible speaks about and from the Christianity that I had experienced. From what I knew the bible spoke about and what I had seen in Africa, a Christian's life should be very different than the life of unbelievers. Born again children of God should live lives worthy of their calling. Their lives should be living sacrifices and their faith should effect every area of their lives. So many people who I met, who claimed to be Christians, seemed to be living defeated lives that served the world and the flesh, not the true living God.

Soon I met a wonderful lady named Connie McKeen, who encouraged me to write this book. I told her I had some stories in my notebook and was not sure if anyone would understand my English or my handwriting. She offered to type it for me. I was scared to tell someone my whole story, but she showed up at my house, and my wife gave her the handwritten book. Then she surprised me on my birthday with a very well-typed manuscript, along with a digital copy of the book. That gave me hope to finish my work.

Now I thank God that He challenged me to go through the experience of writing this book, because not only did I survive the painful retelling, but it brought healing and freedom. I trust He will use it to do a great work in your life, as well.

Imana iguhe umugisha! (May God give you blessings!)

INTRODUCTION

The beautiful, mountainous country Rwanda is a small land nestled into the edge of Eastern Africa. It is surrounded by the much larger nations of Uganda to the north, Tanzania to the east, the Democratic Republic of the Congo to the west, and the similarly small country of Burundi to the south.

It is not a country of great power or wealth. Many people around the world do not even know it exists or would not have known it existed if it were not for its horrific past. However, it is also a country of rich culture and great natural beauty. It stands out in Eastern Africa as a gem, rare and breathtakingly gorgeous. The hills of Rwanda are green and lush. The climate of Rwanda is perfect year round with temperatures around eighty degrees Fahrenheit. The people of Rwanda are gentle, kind and always hospitable.

Three main tribes of peoples have dominated the recent history of Rwanda: the Hutu, the Tutsi, and the Twa. Although anthropologists disagree on the origins of these people groups, oral history tells of these peoples living in harmony for hundreds of years. The Hutu and the Tutsi were not originally tribes, but social castes. The Tutsi were the rich, ruling class and the Hutu were their servants. If a Tutsi lost wealth, they could then become Hutu and likewise, if the Hutu gained wealth, they could become Tutsi. The Twa were a mostly separate undeveloped people that usually lived in the forests of Rwanda.

Rwanda was first colonized by the Germans and then later changed hands to the Belgians in 1916 as a result of World War I. In 1935, the Belgians instituted the system of identity cards distinguishing Hutu from Tutsi and therefore creating two separate, immovable tribes. They carved out an elite minority of the country and called them Tutsi. Everyone that was left, was dubbed Hutu. Rwandans were evaluated according to height, intelligence, wealth and their similarity to a European appearance, even having the width of their noses measured. Many believed that this was done to give the Belgians a better hand of control from within Rwanda.

The Tutsi, who were already in power, were then locked into positions of authority by the identity cards. The Hutu were locked into positions of lower class and servitude by the issuance of the identity cards with no way to advance their status. Naturally a huge rift began to grow between the Hutu and the Tutsi. Animosity and resentment then began to grow where there was once a common brotherhood.

In 1959, the Hutu revolted and assumed power, slaughtering thousands of Tutsi and forcing over one hundred thousand to flee Rwanda to neighboring countries. The tables were now turned with only the Hutu being able to hold positions of authority and the Tutsi being shamed and looked down upon. Rwanda then gained its independence with the Hutu in charge.

The Tutsi were often forced into the forests of Rwanda and largely discriminated against. Over the decades, the children of the exiled Tutsi along with similar minded Hutu began to form an army in Uganda with hopes of bringing Rwanda back to the peace it knew before it was colonized. This army was called the Rwandan Patriotic Front (RPF).

After years of training and preparation, the RPF invaded Rwanda in 1990 as a unified, determined force. Although this army was small compared to the national Hutu led army of the Rwandan government, they posed as serious threat. A civil war then ensued in Rwanda until a cease fire agreement was signed in 1993 as part of the Arusha Peace Talks.

The peace talks continued into 1994, giving the international community the image of a healing Rwanda. However, the Hutu power extremists in the government had other plans. While they were undergoing peace talks and appearing cooperative to the world, behind closed doors, they were preparing for a mass slaughter of every Rwandan Tutsi.

On April 6, 1994 the plane carrying Juvénal Habyarimana, president of Rwanda, was shot down, thus ending the cease fire between the RPF and the Rwandan national army. Over the next one hundred days, over one million Tutsi and moderate Hutu were tortured and slaughtered. The international community watched the genocide happen and chose not to intervene. Many of the U.N. peacekeeping forces put in place before the mass violence began in Rwanda were actually pulled out of the country. Those that were left were instructed not to intervene. The killings were finally put to an end by mid July when the RPF gained control of the country.

It is during this period between the beginning of President Juvénal Habyarimana's administration and the violence that ensued following his assassination that my story begins.

CHAPTER 1
MY EARLY YEARS

HOME AND CHORES

I was born in Rukumbeli in the county of Sake in the province of Kibungo (now called the Eastern Province) of Rwanda around 1980. Although Rwanda is the land of a thousand hills, Sake is mostly flat land covered in small villages.

Rukumbeli was full of mud brick houses. Each house had an extensive private garden because the gardens supported the families. It was their only resource since there were no other jobs to be had.

When my parents were younger, the Tutsi were put there by the government. After the genocide of 1959, many Tutsi fled their homes and had nowhere else to go. At that time, Rukumbeli was all forest, full of the deadly tsetse fly. The government gave the land to the Tutsis as a place to settle. Then they were left there to die. The flies remained and were a plague among my people. Over the years, the Tutsi cut down the forests to get rid of the flies, so by the time I was born, the threat was gone.

I was a young boy with good parents who raised me until I was fourteen years old. I had many dreams, just like other kids. I was one of the happiest boys in my village. I was content with what we had and loved the community around us.

The fifth of eight children, I had five brothers and two sisters. These were our names in order of birth: Ephrem, Shyaka,

Mukashyaka, Jean Marie Vianney, Theoneste (Theo), Felicien, Christine, Emmanuel.

I woke up most of the time at 5:00 or 5:30 a.m. with my brothers. Our father always had hard work for us to do on our small farm. Many times we pulled weeds from among the banana trees or pressed the juice out of the bananas. Then we would walk down to Lake Mugesera to bring water for banana beer or for cooking lunch. It was a long walk. The way back home was uphill, which made it a lot harder. All of this had to be done between five o'clock and eight o'clock each morning.

OUR SCHOOL

Then off to school we went. Our school was about one kilometer (a little over half a mile) away. It was built of mud bricks and had a sheet-metal roof and a dirt floor. There was no electricity or running water.

When I was younger, every student was supposed to bring a gallon of water from the lake each morning. This was poured onto the floor to settle the dust and keep away the small red insects that burrowed into our feet and laid their eggs. The larva would grow under our skin, causing injuries and deformation of our feet if not removed. To get them out, we used needles. It was painful, but not difficult to do. We had the same bugs in our homes, but we could not afford shoes to protect our feet. If the ground was kept wet, however, they would not come. When I was around fourteen years old, the government built a better school with hard floors.

School was so torturous for us; the teachers made us work like slaves. Our schools had no janitors, so the students were required to clean everything and tend the grounds. We swept the floors daily and mopped a few times a week. Many schools planted gardens to sell the produce for extra money. The students worked the gardens too. We never saw any of the food we helped to grow. We were sent home for lunch because the government could not afford to feed us. They beat us like cows, especially if we came even one minute late without a good excuse.

It was very common in Rwanda for teachers to carry a staff to punish any mistake made by students. Tusti were more closely watched and punished more often. As a young child I did not understand why some of my classmates would seem to be favored by the teacher and others were treated so poorly, but as I got older, I began to understand.

Our tribe was often excluded from various activities, such as soccer, which was the most popular game in Africa. We had soccer championships in our province, but if a team was from a Tutsi region, which of course would be Tutsi team, the arbiter would favor the Hutu team to make sure they won. It was often through violence. If a Tutsi got kicked in the leg it would be okay as long as there was no revenge. As in school, the Tutsi were watched more closely and punished more severely. Very often the Tutsi would get frustrated with the situation and retaliate with violence within the game. Many times the games ended with fights.

My tribe was smart in school, but the leaders would change our names on the national tests and give our scores to their own children to get them into high school. In that area, we gave up.

The headmaster and leaders of the school were all Hutu, although the teachers could be of either background. It was the lucky Tutsi who was allowed to teach since we were not able to hold positions of leadership. The teachers spoke harshly to terrify us and because of hatred. It was a system of dictatorship in which we were expected to follow their lead without discussion. The Hutu administrators were the ones who decided whether we passed the national test and moved on the next grade. Although we Tutsi would pass every test, when it came to the national exams, only the Hutu went through.

We all had to pay fees to attend school. It was a huge burden on most families to come up with these fees. We had no textbooks. There were drawing slates that we purchased at the market to practice our writing. When we were old enough to write, we had to buy notebooks to copy the lessons that our teachers printed on the blackboard.

We always said that our last year of education was primary six, and then we would try to work on our farms or create our own jobs to survive. All my older brothers stopped after primary six, except the oldest, Ephrem, who attended a private secondary school and then worked for his school fees all by himself. Because he was so smart, he was able to pass the tests after several months out of school, working to pay his fees. The other students hated him and tried to kill him many times, but he always escaped. The Hutu students who were jealous of him used to set traps to hurt him. Some of them whose fathers were involved in the military were more corrupt and sometimes carried guns with them. He was too smart though and never allowed himself to be put in a situation where he could be attacked.

FREE TIME

That was normal school life for us. My favorite time was after school on my way home, playing soccer with the other kids. The soccer ball was always homemade from tightly wrapped banana leaves or plastic bags. Soccer was our culture; we even had competitions between classes, towns, and different provinces. I also loved to do gymnastics and was good at it.

I played with our neighbors and kids in our village a lot. We were free from a young age to wander around our village. There wasn't any danger of us being kidnapped or hurt by strangers like there is in America and much of the West now. Our parents didn't worry when they didn't know where we were. We were often gone all day, free to do what we wanted, when school was not in session.

My brother Vianney was my closest friend, but we were very competitive and often fought a lot. Our fights could get physical, and we often hurt each other, but no bitterness remained between us. I used to play soccer with all my brothers, but especially with Vianney. We worked together in a lot of things, like fetching water and gathering wood. Even though we fought a lot, if anyone came between us, we would beat them together.

Sometimes I played with my brother Felicien, who was two years younger, but not for very long. He was always running off on his own, trying to figure out how things worked and inventing new things. He was so clever. He studied the world around him and often figured out how to fool others. Sometimes he would do something bad and knew that he would be in trouble when my father got home, so he would hide among us to go unnoticed by my father. He hid himself in such a way that he could not be seen even when he was among us. Sometimes he even escaped punishment this way. I remember one night he feared punishment from my father so he took off running as fast as he could. When we saw how fast he ran, we all worried about him, fearing he would get hurt in the forest at night. We all went looking for him and spent an hour or more looking. Finally we found him in the house. He had taken off running super fast so that we would think he went far, but really he ran and hid around the corner of our house. He watched us looking for him the whole time. When we discovered what really happened, we all laughed so hard that my father forgot about punishing him.

Felicien was so quiet but busy with his own things. He was always the last to fall asleep and the first to wake up. We used to say that even when he was asleep, he was listening. He made many toys out of nothing. He believed bigger than he could afford. Felicien was never terrified but thought he could overcome anything.

My younger sister, Christine, had a special place in my heart. She was so funny and always so full of life. If I was having a bad day, she was the one I wanted to be around with. She was so adorable, we used to pray she would never grow up. She seemed to encourage others just by being near them. Whenever she figured out something new, she made sure everyone else was informed. We laughed and laughed at her because she was so talkative and said the funniest things. Christine was so special in our family. She was the only young girl, because Mukashyaka was so much older, and she was surrounded with brothers. My brothers and I used to play rough with each other, but we always made sure that she was safe and taken care of. If we were in America, we would have called her our princess.

We had to make sure there was water and firewood in the morning and after school. Once that was taken care of, we were free to run. When it started to get dark, it was time to be home. After dinner we sometimes went straight to bed. Other times we went to a neighbor's house to listen to stories on the radio. Sometimes we played games by the light of the moon. My favorite times were when neighbors would get together to play music, and we danced our traditional dance.

OUR COMMUNITY

In town, there was an open-air market, selling food and used clothing. There were also small boutiques that sold lamp oil, matches, notebooks, soap, warm soda, and other necessities. The market was available only on Wednesdays and Saturdays. If I did not get what I wanted then, I had to get it at the boutiques. But it was better to shop at the open-air markets since prices were cheaper and there was a wider selection.

The air was filled with the smell of fruits, spices, fish and meat cooking over a fire. It was full of life and engaged my senses. As we walked through the market, people would call out, advertising their products and services. Sometimes the sellers would hire specialized yellers to advertise their products.

We recognized their voices before we even entered the market: "Twenty! Twenty! We got pants for twenty! I'll accept twenty today!" they would yell out. "Fifty! Fifty! Special price just for today!"

Sometimes we would go to buy. Sometimes we went to sell, bringing beans, bananas, and any other fruits that we had in abundance. We would stay to sell our produce ourselves, or we would sell it to others to resell if we did not want to stay all day. Usually my older siblings would go to the market for my family. Sometimes I got to go with them, but most of the time I only went to follow my mother around and carry the things she purchased for our family.

There was no electricity or running water in our village, not even in the boutiques. At night the flickering flames of oil lamps lit our village.

At harvest time, one family would make wine and take thirty to sixty gallons to a neighbor as a gift to confirm their friendship. All the other neighbors were invited, and the wine was usually consumed right then at the party.

The older men would sit around and discuss life. Many of the elders were in their eighties and nineties, but most of them were between forty-five and sixty. Sometimes one man would stand up and announced that he was going to give a cow to another. Everyone clapped and cheered. A cow was an honored gift, which meant that they would be friends for life.

We lived together in community. Older men and women were aunts and uncles to us. The village was like one family. Although I belonged to my parents, as children, we belonged to the village as well. Our character and actions could be corrected by any adult in the village and we had to listen to them out of respect. When young men took a wife, she would be presented to the whole village and they gathered together and celebrated the addition of a new daughter to the family.

We did life together. It was customary for the men of my village to gather together for fellowship. It was in these times of fellowship that our community's "government" was established. Rules and standards were discussed as our fathers drank local wine and mulled over the important matters of our lives.

The women of our village family spent much time together as well. It was normal for neighbors to help with the keeping of each other's houses. Laundry was washed together; harvested crops were prepared together and household goods were shared.

If someone ever broke into your house to steal from your family, the whole village would show up to defend you at the sound of the first screams. They surrounded the house to make sure the thief was caught and brought to justice.

MY PARENTS

Thieves that were caught were often brought to my father. He was the punisher. He would beat the thieves severely and then tell them how they had to compensate for their crime. We had no local police, but we had no need for them. Punishments and repayments were handled by the leaders in the village.

My mother and father were also local healers. Often people came to my parents to have them treat their ailments with natural cures. If they had a sickness that the doctors could not treat, people expected my mother and father to treat them.

My father was a proud, strong man of much wisdom. He was respected in the whole community. Only Hutu could hold public office, but my father had a great deal of influence anyway. The people looked to him even though he held no official position.

Before the genocide, the elders of our village knew something was coming. Sometimes we heard rumors that the Hutu were coming. The men of the village gathered at my father's home. He organized them into groups and assigned them areas to protect.

My mother was a strong woman. She worked hard to take care of me and my siblings. Women in Rwanda were not like women in the Western world. They hardly ever cried or showed emotion. They did not cuddle their children or show them much affection. My mother never hugged or kissed me, but I knew she loved me, even if she never told me.

In our culture, it was not proper to eat from food as it was being prepared. You did not snack. We had lunch and dinner. That's it. There was no breakfast. I used to be so hungry all the time and could never get enough to eat. My mother knew it, and she would sneak food to me between mealtimes. That's how I knew she loved me. Sometimes she even left sweet potatoes in a pot for me in the morning.

Although she did not show emotions, she was a woman of compassion. At times our family struggled to buy food. My mother could not bear to tell us that she had no food for us, so she would put a pan of water on the fire as if she was going to cook something in it. Then she would tell us to go to bed and said she would wake us up when dinner was ready. Of course, we were never awakened because there was no food for us to eat. I knew she couldn't stand to see the pain on our faces if she told us there was no food.

Much of the time we ate well, especially during harvest. We had a large plot of land with a lot planted on it. We had mango, avocado, and banana trees, pineapple plants, sorghum, passion fruit, sweet potatoes, and much more. I remember some days I ate a lunch of avocados. I climbed up into a tree to pick and eat avocados until I was full. I often ate six or more in one sitting, and I ate mangoes the same way.

Although there are many things I treasure from my culture and the way I was raised, there were also things I know were not honoring to God or healthy. For one, it is part of our culture to label children with certain names. I was called something that meant "stupid animal." Because Rwanda is a high-context culture, differences in people were often not accepted. I was very smart as a boy, but always did things differently, so I was considered stupid even though I got the highest scores in my class. Learning came to me so easily. My teachers were so impressed with me, especially in French. Even though I did well, many did not want to accept that I could be smart. It was mostly outside of school that I was looked down on and called stupid names.

My head was usually in the clouds, and I was often lost in thought. That is why my father called me stupid. I was always dreaming of the future. One time my mother told me to go to the neighbor's to get an ax, I became distracted on the way and forgot what I was supposed to get. Sometimes I forgot what house I had been sent to, or I brought my mother back a knife instead of an ax.

In Rwanda, it was the custom at the end of the school year to invite the parents and present the children that were moving up in order of their scores. They lined us up from first place all the way to the poor child who got the lowest scores in the last place. One year, three other children and I were tied for first place. When we were called to take our places, they called me first. One of the other boys who had tied with me stood before me in the line. I told him to move and let me be first because the teacher had called me first. He said it did not matter because we were both first. We continued to argue about it and started to fight in front of all the parents. My father watched the whole thing, laughing and beaming with pride.

My teacher said, "Okay, Theo, I did call you first. Go ahead and take the first place."

My father was so proud, but when we got home, he asked how it was possible for me to get first place. "How could such a stupid boy do so well in school?"

I was so confused. I thought I was stupid because my father told me so. I didn't know how it was possible for a stupid boy like me to get first place.

My parents and neighbors used to call me names and confess bad words to me until I really felt stupid. I couldn't believe in myself anymore. During my entire childhood, I used to believe other guys were much smarter than me, even when I got the top grade in my school. I never believed anything good could come from me.

Despite the troubles I faced, my life in Rukumbeli was good. I loved the simplicity of life and the bonds in our community. I often look back and long for a time like this again. Although there was definitely tension between the Hutu and Tutsi, for much of my childhood I did not understand it. When I was younger, I didn't even know which tribe I belonged to.

As I entered my teens I began to understand more. I started to make sense of the favoritism I saw. My parents began to speak more to me as well about the tribal conflict. Although I was starting to comprehend the danger around us, I never imagined we would face a horror as monumental as the one that was being planned for us.

CHAPTER 2
RUNNING FOR OUR LIVES

THE BEGINNING OF THE END

On Wednesday, April 6, around 6:00 p.m., President Habyarimana Juvenal's airplane was landing at Kanombe International Airport, but before the plane touched down, it was shot and burned. Rwandan president Habyarimana Juvenal and Burundian president Cyprian Ntaryamira, who was riding with him from a meeting in Tanzania, were killed.

No one found out who shot the airplane. The whole government, dominated by the Hutu, blamed the Tutsi for the shooting. It was also said that Mr. Juvenal and his government were preparing to start the genocide soon since people were already trained and had tools that had been provided by the nation of France and Rwandan leadership. It seemed to some that Juvenal was losing his control of the government, and his death was used as a ploy for the extremists, who held most of the power in the government, to begin their planned ethnic cleansing.

The next day, Thursday, April 7, I woke up as usual and went downtown to sell our homemade beer at the market to get some money for the family. That was my task for the day. Before I left, everyone in town was joining his or her neighbor who had a radio to listen to the news about our president.

My mom warned me to be careful, even though everyone was happy about a dictator who was defeated. Her view was different. She told me that this was the biggest tragedy we had to face.

The phrase "The tall trees have fallen" began blaring repeatedly from the radio, signaling to all Hutu that the time had come to wipe the Tutsi from the face of the earth. Every Hutu in our neighborhood was ready as the national radio station began to announce clearly that all Tutsi must be killed and that they were to make sure no one survived.

Around 9:00 a.m., no one was in town to buy anything. It didn't take long for the market to empty. Tutsi fled in fear, and Hutu raced for their weapons. I took off and went back home. Every Tutsi in my village was shaken and terrified by the news. The Hutu were ready to kill us all and take our possessions.

We gathered together in one place as Tutsi to see what would happen next. No one could eat. No one could sleep. No one could work. Life stopped. Life as we knew it had ended. Every hour the situation grew worse. They announced on the national radio the names of prominent Tutsi who were already dead. They also encouraged all trained groups of Hutu, such as the Interahamwe, police and military, to go help local Hutu civilians to kill all the rest of the Tutsi.

This first day seemed to last forever. Minutes stretched into hours, and hours seemed like weeks. We were frozen in fear and disbelief. Sometime in the afternoon, my dad came home, running from a huge group of Hutu with guns and machetes in their hands. He was scared. That was the first time in my life I saw my dad afraid. I felt fear pierce straight into the core of me.

We all ran with him to hide in the bush and among the sorghum trees. No one was able to go back home, but we hid all night. The next day, my dad and other brave men organized themselves for battle, with kids like me behind them, carrying stones in our bags to support our fathers. The arrangement was that if they withdrew, they would find those stones gathered on the street, and then they could use them to defend themselves.

We did this for about two-and-a-half weeks. We were able to defend ourselves quite successfully at that time, with only a handful of lives lost. Then came the military, Interahamwe, and all the Hutu civilians armed with all kinds of tools to kill us.

THURSDAY CALLED THE END

I first heard noises early in the morning before the sun came up. We were in one of the uncovered houses, where we met every evening to see how many survived the day. Because there were so many of us together, and it was so wet and rainy outside, there was not even room for everyone to lie down. Many nights I had to sleep standing up.

We heard the shout of machine guns and the noise of men and women. It was hard to know what kind of noise it was because Hutu were killing people in torturous ways. They said that this Thursday was "the end of the Tutsi tribe." They chopped people into pieces before they died. Men and women were tortured naked on the street. They removed the eyes of some and ordered them to run. They cut the legs and arms off of others and forced them to eat their own flesh. Some were burned to death in houses, and some abused sexually with pieces of wood and knives. They were commanded to take women who were pregnant and cut open their bellies to take the babies out to be killed before their mothers.

Hutu women came with their husbands to kill Tutsi babies. They picked up the babies and hit them on walls to smash their heads. Some infants were crushed in wheat presses. The Burundian Hutu came along with Rwandan Hutu to teach them how to kill in torturous ways.

That day was so miserable for all of us. We lost thousands, and many were still bleeding and asking for help. They bled and cried for a week because the Hutu said that the best way to kill Tutsis was to make them suffer for at least three days. We had no way to help them; all we could do was run to protect our own lives.

But my life that day was miraculous.

Shortly after I heard the noises, we were attacked, and everyone fled in different directions. As I fled, I met two other boys running for their lives. One was around five years older than me, and the other was about five years younger. The older boy, Muvoma, was more terrified than anyone I had ever seen before. They both said that they wanted to stay with me and wouldn't go, so I asked them to hide with me among the banana trees.

There were about ten banana trees growing in a circle (see picture of the group of banana trees for reference). We sat down and made them our shelter. That morning was rainier than any other day I can remember. As we hid among the banana trees, in the midst of my fear, I was distracted by the rain. That morning was rainier than any other day I can remember. The rain fell like buckets drenching us as we tried to run and creating thick mud around us as we tried to hide.

Soon, there came a long line of killers with hammers, machetes, guns, and other tools that they made just for killing us. They walked slowly and quietly until they reached our banana trees. We heard them tell each other that the trees would be a good place for their prey to hide. I reached for a banana leaf and cut it with my hand to try and cover my group, but the Hutu decided to search inside or cut the trees down. I was wearing a red coat and cursed it for its bright color. I said, "God, I don't know about promises. I don't think You're concerned about me, and if You can't help me, it's okay. I am dying, and I don't know what to do."

One of the killers shouted to the others that he had seen us, so they threw a spear at us. It hit Muvoma. I heard him groan a little before I took off running. I turned around and ran again into the mud street, slipping, while the other boy followed me. I knew the older boy was dead, but Emmanuel, the younger boy, was right behind me as we ran together. I never understood why they could see hope in me when I thought I had none.

In a couple hundred meters, we found ourselves right in front of a big group armed to kill; then we turned around and ran back the way we had come. They sent one soldier to kill us, but God was right between me and that soldier, even though I didn't see Him.

As I ran from the soldier trying to shoot me, there was a song playing so loudly in my mind that it was all I could think of. I had heard it on the radio, but I did not understand what it meant. I knew that it was a prayer, but the truth of the promise within was not clear to me. This song stayed with me throughout the genocide constantly playing in my mind as a promise from the Lord.

> Wasezeranye ngo dusabe tuzahabwa
> ngo nidukomange tuzakingurirwa
> (You promised that if we ask it shall be given unto us.
> If we knock the door shall be open unto us.)

Looking back now, I know that God put it there as my prayer for help, and He surely was with me. I knew He was there because as this soldier took his aim at me, I was untouched by any bullet. They fired again and again, and we were unharmed.

Then before my eyes crossed a man with a bow in his hand. His name was Dominic, and he was one of our mighty men of war. He had been fighting skillfully and bravely for us for several weeks. But his life was running short. When the soldier recognized him, he signaled to the others, and they followed him. It was raining so hard as they followed him. I ran behind the soldier who had failed to kill me, while a big group of killers was running behind me. I saw Dominic fall and struggle to get up again.

Spotting a tall bush, I jumped into it to hide. From about midday until seven hours later, I lay there in almost perfect stillness. I dared not move my head or any other part of my body for fear that the sound would give me away.

That evening, the whole village was so quiet. It seemed like everyone was dead. Bodies covered the ground like a blanket. I searched among them to find anyone breathing. I walked all over, stepping on lifeless bodies.

As soon as I reached the street, there was a big group of Hutu with animals they had stolen from the village. I tried to hide myself behind a small bush on the street. There was an old man standing in that street near me, hopeless and, I think, believing there was no reason for him to live anymore. As I hid behind the bush, they seized him and chopped him until I felt his blood moving toward me like a flood. One of the animals ran from them in my direction. When they chased after it, I lay down like a dead person until they disappeared from that place.

I knew they were going back to their homes, for it was getting darker. I raised my head to see if anyone else was still alive. There were two men walking with bows in their hands. One was Dominic, the warrior; the other was his friend, Rukara, who was also brave in battle. I walked with them over the whole village, trying to see if we could find anyone else alive. We found a few, but most of them were badly injured. They called our names, asking for help, but unfortunately there was no help to provide. Many of them were killed in the next two or three days or died from loss of blood.

We went back to our meeting place. There I found both my parents, my four brothers—Ephrem, Shyaka, Felecien, and baby Emmanuel (who was about a year old)—and my little sister Christine. However, two were still missing, and no one knew what had happened to them. These were my big sister, Jeanne d'Arc, who was kidnapped, and my brother Vianney, who left the town long before the genocide started. He lived far away, and we had no hope that he would survive.

That day, thousands of people died in that place. I understand when I read Psalm 91:7, which says thousands will die in your sight, and nothing will happen to you, or the promises in Isaiah 43 about God's protection. That Thursday evening I began to believe the promise in Matthew 7:7.

The next day, Friday, was quiet and very confusing. The killers thought we were all dead and didn't attack us. Yet we stayed in fear all day, waiting for another surprise attack. We were safe that day and then started a fire to cook some food. Unbeknownst us, the killers saw the smoke and began planning another attack.

SATURDAY: THE UNFORGETTABLE

We were all up and waiting early the next morning for whatever was to come. We waited until early afternoon when the attack began. Some of our men tried to fight the Hutu, and within a few minutes, they ran away as if defeated. Our men ran after them and killed one.

The next time the Hutu came, they had a strategy. At the back of their group was our mayor with a machine gun. When they started the fight, we tried to fight back, but then they moved over to the sides to give him room to shoot. We were terrified because we had never seen a gun like that before. We ran away, and all the civilian Hutu with their machetes ran after us and killed many people on that field. There were many women with children in their arms and old people who could not run.

They all entered a house. The Hutu burned it and stood outside so that if anyone tried to escape, they were killed with machetes.

My mom told me that she wanted to die with them, but I urged her to run with me. She wasn't able to run well, for she was holding baby Emmanuel, and there was nowhere to escape. Soon she stopped and told me to run as much as I could, but I didn't want to leave her there. She yelled at me to run, but I insisted that I would not leave her. It seemed like that moment lasted forever, but I know it must have been only seconds. I saw so many Hutu coming toward us, killing everyone they caught.

She screamed, "Keep running! I see life in you. Run and never give up." She knew I would survive, but I had to run and not stop running.

There was nothing I could do to protect her, but still I couldn't abandon her. I think it is natural for boys to feel like they need to protect their mothers. I always thought nothing would ever happen to my mom.

That moment I had to make a painful decision and follow her prophecy as she continued to plead with me. "Theo, run. Please run. You must survive. Just keep running."

That was the last time I heard my mother's voice. I pretended for many years that I didn't know what happened to my mother and baby Emmanuel, but I saw the big group of Hutu move in on them as I ran.

Before too long, I found my little sister Christine, who was about six years old, wandering around and confused in the middle of the noise and killing. She grabbed my hand, and we ran together. As we crossed the road, we came to Lake Mugesera, where many people tried to drown themselves to escape the torture of the Hutu. We didn't say anything to each other as we faced the large group of Hutu with spears, knives, and guns covered in the blood of our families.

She turned to the left and tore herself out of my hand because of fear. I don't remember how it felt when her hand withdrew from mine. I was so frozen in fear, I couldn't move. I let her go, and I never saw her again. That was my biggest failure in life, to not be able to keep my little sister alive. For that reason I hated living after the genocide. I continued to judge myself because I gave up on her.

With nowhere to go, I just ran in a circle around the houses. The killers were too many, and I had nowhere to hide. I tried to run between them to get to the lake until I found myself very close to many killers covered in our blood standing by the shore.

They signaled to each other about me saying, "There is that snake. Get him."

That was me, a snake.

I turned around, remembering the words my mother spoke over me that I had to keep running if I was to survive. I ran for a bit and then stopped, not knowing where to go. How could there be any hope for me to survive? There was nowhere to flee. Everyone was falling, cut to pieces in front of me. Surely I was next.

I was caught in the middle of the killers. I don't know how to describe their moves, their techniques, or their look. What I saw in their eyes was pure evil. Even though I had never seen the devil before, it was clear that he was acting through these killers. They had machetes and spears that were very tall and bloody. They wore uniforms that had many colors, but by this time, they were completely stained in the blood that they had shed.

There was a house on fire, with many dead bodies in front of the door. I jumped in among the flames. The ceiling had collapsed, and some walls inside were also down. Although the flames were gone, I could see the burning embers, as the walls still glowed like charcoal. When I entered, I had one wish—to die by the fire instead of their swords and prayed, "God, I don't know if you are real, but even if you are, surely you are not able to save me here, and I understand that. So please now, take my life painlessly and take me to heaven." I knew there was a heaven and hell. The song of promise that never left me during the genocide repeated inside me again and again, louder and louder.

A few minutes later one group of killers came to see if someone was in the house because they saw my footprints in the ashes. The commander told one of his men to go in and get me. As I listened, my heart beat overtime, and I could hear its pounding from my chest. One guy tried to enter the building and was burned.

I questioned the song in my heart again. Then I thought, if somebody actually said those words, he has to be powerful.

I said in my heart, *God, if You are real and You can hear me, please pay attention to me. I am dying right now, and I would like to ask You to spare my life again, but it's impossible. Please open the door since that is what the next part of the song says: "Knock and the door shall be opened unto you."*

I was sitting on the floor, hiding behind the broken section of a wall that was just big enough to conceal someone of my size. I leaned on the outer wall, ready to die. Once the guy sent to kill me entered the house, I stretched my neck and closed my eyes, just to be sure that he had a good shot at making a clean slice on my neck. That way, I would die quicker, even though that wasn't their intention. He walked in carefully and reached the section of wall I was leaning on from the other side. He stood so close I could see his feet. I quickly raised my prayer in this emergency. *God, here I come, and I know You can't save me, but You said something about knocking. Please, I don't want to go to hell.* As soon as he touched the wall, the killer screamed loudly, "Fire! Fire! Fire!" Then he turned around before he could spot me. and told the other men that if anybody was in the house, they would have surely died because the walls were like burning coals and glowed red hot.

These prayers were from a confused young boy who knew nothing about the power of God or even God himself. I was only hoping somebody could hear me and save me.

The walls and roof of the house were already down. It would have been easy to see me, but God blinded them.

What a mighty God to whom we pray! I thought He didn't care about sinners, but now I know his mercy is beyond our wishes. He sees us all as His children, no matter what we think about Him.

This time I thought I was dreaming, or dead already, because the fear in me wouldn't even let me think. That group decided that the fire had killed me already. They left in a hurry to kill everyone else before the sun went down. This was the last day to finish—or so they thought.

I don't know the reason God chose to let me live, but He did. I know many people who were stronger and who could do mighty works of God, but He chose me. When I get to heaven, I will ask Him why, because it doesn't make a lot of sense.

I see now that He had put his word in my heart through the song I had heard, and it had power that carried me through my time of desperate need. I praise the Lord that He chose to intervene in my life and teach me the power of His promises and His word.

The hours passed, and I was still sitting there, filled with fear and confusion. I could not believe that the promise of God may have worked for me. I wondered if that promise was for someone like me or just for those who had sung the song. Can a simple prayer save you from the fire? I don't even know if I was saved by my prayer. I only know that God saved me by His grace, and I believe that every word He says is true.

As I continued to question and test God's existence, the Lord continued to prove Himself to me. In a few hours, another group came. I was so afraid. I heard the cries of children and adults being tortured behind the house I was hiding in. The killers stopped and checked in the ashes. Finding footprints on the floor, they decided to come in and check whether anyone was hiding in the house.

This time there was no fire or any sign of it. The house was very small, and I could hear everything they said. We were separated only by one wall.

As they stood there trying to decide who would go in, their commander came and saw them. I heard him yelling at them with much authority, "What do you think you are doing, lazy people. Don't you know the work we have today? Move, now."

That moment I survived again.

After they left, I came out to see what had been happening. I saw a young boy in front of the house. He was about three years old. He was injured, and he couldn't walk, so he lay down as if he was dead. When he saw me, he stared speechless, maybe hoping that I could do something. There was nothing to do. I decided to go back inside and sit down at the same place to wait for the night, as usual.

Finally, as I continued to question if there was a God, I heard another group running toward the house. As I listened intently, I heard that they were chasing a chicken. They were such a greedy people; they wanted to leave nothing behind.

They stopped right at the house and saw the same footprints in the ashes. The chicken flew over the house trying to fall in, and they were going to come in following that animal, and that would have been the end of my life. When the chicken saw me, it got scared and flew back out to the other side.

While others were discussing whether to come in, the boy sneezed. One of the killers said, "Oh, this is the one, and he is not dead."

Right then I heard the sound of a machete cutting into the boy; I could hear the blood gushing from his neck. They killed this three-year-old child who was lying on his dead mother. He died in my place. It was late in the evening, and they thought everyone was dead.

This happened to me at least three times, and God spared my life. I had sat in the house, surrounded by the burning walls, and was neither burned nor even felt warmth from the fire for hours.

I didn't feel like God had saved me right away, but my spirit was challenged somehow. All I needed was for someone to explain what had just happened to me. However, everyone there had his or her own stories, so I told no one about it. There was no one to explain anything about God.

Later in the evening, I came out of the house and saw the desolation. Covering the ground were the dead bodies of my friends, relatives and neighbors. Among all of the bodies blanketing the earth, one little boy stood out to me. He was the one that I had heard them attack. I saw that they had slit his throat, but he was still alive, bleeding. He was breathing and still looking at me. I knew he was going to die soon, and there was nothing I could do to help him. I walked away, knowing that he had died in my place.

I looked around, trying to find whoever survived to stay with. I met my older brother Ephrem with another couple, a man and his pregnant wife, with whom we stayed until our village was liberated.

The Hutus were supported by Sylvan Mutabaruka, the mayor of our district, the man armed with a machine gun. The rest of the civilians involved in the killing had machetes and clubs with nails protruding from them. On that traumatizing day, I saw ladies abused sexually, mothers cut to pieces, and pregnant women cut open so that killers could take their babies out to dash them on walls, trees, and swords.

As we walked a bit further, we came upon the worst situation we had ever seen, and everyone's heart melted. There were hundreds of people lying on the ground crying for help because the killers said that we should die in pain, and they saw to it that many did. Men, women, and children covered the ground, having had their arms or legs severed or with huge machete gashes in their heads or other parts of their bodies. They were still alive, but mutilated. They begged all who passed by to kill them quickly and end their misery, but we couldn't bring ourselves to do it. To kill them would have been to become like those that had been possessed by a spirit more evil than we ever imagined.

My brother and I walked around looking for survivors. Most of the Tutsi in the area had already been killed. Little by little, we found maybe 350 who were still alive. As soon as everyone gathered, my dad began to address the survivors. He told them of his plan to escape to our neighboring country, Burundi.

Before we departed, I learned that my dad had to take a gallon of water to my mom, where she was left chopped to pieces, but still breathing. The loss of blood had given many of the mutilated unquenchable thirst and they begged for water. They had cut off her arms and legs and slit her throat, leaving her to bleed out. I knew she was in the same place where I had left her. I couldn't bring myself to go to her.

That night around forty of us—including Ephrem, Shyaka, Felicien, my father and I (the only remaining members of my family)—said good-bye to our loved ones and departed for Burundi. They wished us luck, and then we took off. That night we walked miles and miles. But before we could cross the Akagera River, there was a major roadblock, and we woke the guards by accident. They woke everyone else to follow us, but God was with me still. One man threw a spear at me, and it landed between my legs. I flipped it with my legs into the bush.

As we ran, we were scattered and our group was divided. Then my dad crossed the river with almost half of the group because they knew the way. The rest of us lost our way. My dad and Shyaka, my second oldest brother, were together with half of the team, who were able to cross the river.

Those of us that did not cross the river struggled all night long, wondering where we were—hungry, sleepy and cold in the wet weather of April. We waited for the sun to shine, but it was not good for us because the whole town knew that we were hiding in their farms.

SUNDAY: A DAY OF BLOOD

Sunday morning, the Hutus woke up with a plan. I heard them say they were going to hunt us down and go home to have breakfast and then attend church. They hunted us that whole morning until we were all separated. There we lost my younger brother, Felicien Nsanzimfura, and other cousins.

Later the killers found where I was hiding. They had dogs with them, but I ran away so fast that even their dogs could not catch me. However, it was their place, and they never gave up chasing me.

I found a Christian church that I thought no one would dare to come into to kill me. As soon as I stepped inside, I saw blood all over the walls and on the floor. Finding pieces of flesh scattered around, as well, I knew there was no hope of taking shelter in that building. I stepped out quickly and hid in the bush behind it. Later I learned that the pastor was Hutu, and he invited his entire congregation to come and hide in the church. After all the Tutsis in his congregation were inside, he called his team of killers, who came and slaughtered them all. I don't know of any who survived that massacre—around two thousand people lost their lives.

That day I walked back to the place where the survivors used to gather, so I could search for anyone else still living. We never walked on the road during this time, but traveled as secretly as we could. However, I gave up when I could not find anyone else alive and began walking on the road where everybody could see me.

I even talked to some of the killers, who asked me where I was coming from and where I was going. I lied to them, as if I was in peace, and they responded as if nothing had been happening. Yet they knew who I was, and they set a trap for me. As we talked, I saw in the distance some men running on the other side of the bushes to catch me. As they came toward me, I began walking faster. When I saw that they picked up their pace as well, I broke into a run.

I didn't even really want to live at this point and didn't know why I was running. There must have been something deep inside of me that still had hope and clung to life. My mother's words had planted a seed in me that I had to obey. Somehow I managed to escape again.

I was very hungry, and since I was close to my father's land, I looked around his little farm to find anything to eat. It was hopeless. The killers had come and stolen or destroyed everything.

I continued walking. A few hours later, I arrived at the secret meeting place of survivors in Rwamibabi, a Tutsi neighborhood in Rukumbeli. There I found around fifty people still living. We met away from the road where there had been a house that had burned to the ground. It was the home of one of my distant relatives who had died before the killing began, Emile Bwanakeye. His sons lived in the house before it was burned. Two of them were among the survivors, but the property was no longer theirs. As prey, we lost all ownership. Things like that no longer mattered.

Some of them helped me find something to eat, and my strength was restored. That afternoon in Rwamibabi, I was reunited with my brother Ephrem. As far as we knew, we were the only ones left of our family. We did not know if our father or Shyaka were still alive. We sat down together but had no words to say to each other. Although we had gathered together, we were all alone. We wondered where hope could possibly come from, as we stared at the dead bodies of our loved ones all around us.

That night we all slept in the bushes near where Emile's house was before it had been destroyed.

EPHREM'S STORY

When I was growing up, there was discrimination between our two tribes (Hutu and Tutsi), but I never knew it, because no one would tell me. As in many families, my older brothers knew much more than the younger children. They knew of the tension and were ready to defend themselves and our family.

Ephrem Nsazimana was the oldest of my parents' eight children. He worked so hard to be somebody, even though he knew it would be nearly impossible for him to do so because of our tribe. He did well all through primary school, most of the time achieving the highest grades in his classes, but still he was not admitted into high school. Many times the teachers changed the names on exam papers so that Hutu children could be admitted into high school instead of Tutsi.

But Ephrem never gave up. He left Sake and went to Kigali when he was only fifteen to attend a private secondary school. Private schools were much more expensive, but he paid for it himself by working one semester and going to school the next. He always surprised teachers and students with the way he taught himself and did much better than those who didn't struggle for money.

During the genocide, he fought fearlessly as long as he could. Ephrem was among the older group of boys and men who went ahead of us to fight as me and the other boys my age set the stones in place for them. He never seemed worried at all. I always felt safe when he was around. He was very smart and kept his mind sharp throughout the attack. He had a bow that my father had taught him to use, and he used it well.

Sometimes I would catch a glimpse of him during the day while we all ran our own way, but most of the time I saw him when we gathered at night. In the evenings, when we gathered, he always tried to cheer people up by making jokes about the situation. Sometimes at night, he would sneak to where the Hutu were and listen to their plans for the next day. Then he came back and told us so that we could plan our survival. I never saw him under stress or worried. He gave me hope. I was with him through much of the worst times.

I know that there is much more to be told of Ephrem's experience of the genocide, but I don't know of the details. As a family we have never discussed our own stories and might not ever do so. For many people that experienced great loss in Rwanda, their past is not a place they would like to revisit.

Much of the time Ephrem and I spent together during the slaughter, we didn't talk about what we were experiencing personally. It was too hard to make it real. We had to stay detached from our own personal realities.

That Sunday evening as we sat gathered in our hiding place, something happened that we had never seen or heard before. We heard fighting between the Rwanda Patriotic Front (RPF) and the Hutu government.

We recognized the fight because we began to hear bullets in the air crossing Lake Mugesera. We saw a big group of Hutu in boats crossing the lake, fleeing from the RPF. Our hearts rejoiced, especially the few elders among us. They understood in greater detail what was happening and explained it to us. The truth they shared gave us hope when we thought there could be none.

The Rwanda Patriotic Front was a group of survivors from the genocide of 1959, who had fled from Rwanda into surrounding countries. Fred Rwigema and his team had formed the RPF in Uganda, and the children of the survivors were sent from the countries where they had been displaced to join the army. That night brought some hope, just to know that our God was not killed, as they told us.

Their guns sounded different, and we could tell that their strategy was so much smarter. We knew these people could win the battle, and we hoped they were our rescuers. The next day seemed to be a sure sign that our hope was not in vain.

The Hutu did not come to kill us because they were fleeing for their own lives from the advancing RPF. We could see them in boats rushing to reach the other side of the lake. Many parts of the nation were already taken by the RPF army. That was the end of our lives as the hunted. They no longer came to kill us but were more concerned with the advancing army.

That night we hardly slept because of the thoughts running through our minds. It seemed too good to be true that the nightmare could be over. I didn't know whether to remain in fear or feel relieved. If the RPF were coming, I didn't know if they really would to rescue us.

The next morning, Monday, we were at our gathering place, near the former home of Emile, when my brother Shyaka came, bleeding all over his body. Usually we gathered in groups of five or ten for comfort and I was not in the group that Shayka first approached. Everyone crowded around him with questions of his survival. Some came to tell me that he had arrived. When I heard that he was there, I was so excited to see that he had lived, but sad that he was alone since I knew he had been with my father. I went and joined the group that was listening to his story, but I had missed the first part.

SHYAKA'S STORY

Shyaka had gone all the way to the border of Rwanda and Burundi with my father. There they hid in the Isar forest where cows were kept. In the morning, they were so hungry that they could not continue, and they were not sure of where they were. The group sent Shyaka and his friend Rukara, a bow carrier and a good fighter, to act as spies to see if there was a place to find food. As soon as they came out of the forest, they met a group of farmers carrying guns and swords and were captured alive. They took Shyaka first, hit him and stabbed him from behind with a sword. He pretended that he was dead, but truly could not move since his injuries were so severe.

They then took Rukara and put him beside a big pit where they threw dead bodies. They tortured him with knives and stabbed him in the stomach with swords until he stopped making any sound. Then they came back for Shyaka, picked him up and brought him to the pit. When he saw Rukara lying in the pit, he jumped out and ran for his life.

They followed him most of the evening. When they eventually gave up, he tried to return to Rwamibabi. After three days without food, it was unbelievable that he was able to travel so many miles. He found our father and his group, but soon they were discovered again. He escaped while the rest of his group was killed.

We cooked some sweet potatoes on the fire for him so that he could be revived. We spent the rest of the week together, Shyaka, my oldest brother Ephrem, and me. We hid during the day and came together at night.

Ephrem and Shyaka ran with a group of boys around their age and had many strategies, mostly contrived by Ephrem. When they saw a group of killers coming they would stage a couple of boys in the middle of the road. Meanwhile, Ephrem hid among sorghum plants and made so much noise that the killers would think a small army was approaching them and flee.

CHAPTER 3
DELIVERANCE AND REUNIONS

THE WEEK OF HOPE

After Shyaka came back to us, we continued to hide and watch the fight across Lake Mugesera, hearing the different kinds of gun sounds. The gunfire gave us hope that it would be well with us soon, for we knew there was someone fighting for us against this evil government. Sure enough, that following first week of May, there came news that the RPF was winning the battle and was getting very close to our place.

The Rwandan Patriotic Front had organized after the first Tutsi massacre in 1959, that the Hutu extremists called Revolution 1959, and as a result of Rwandan independence in 1962. They invaded Rwanda on October 1, 1990, led by Fred Rwigema, who lost his life on the second day of the battle. Although the army was discouraged by the loss of their leader, he was soon replaced by Paul Kagame, whose strong leadership rallied the troops with renewed confidence.

By 1994, they had ceased advancement and were in the middle of a long process of peace talks with Habyarimana. However, the talks were a smokescreen to distract the RPF and allow the national army to set up a massive attack. The entire time, Tutsi were being killed, and their annihilation was promoted on the airwaves.

During the peace talks, the RPF were given a place to reside, where six hundred of their soldiers were housed. The strategy

of Habyarimana's army was to confine them in an easily con-
querable location. When the genocide began, that house was the
first attacked. The national army surrounded the building and
opened fire.

What the Hutu did not know was that the RPF understood
the ploy and had made a way for their escape. When they heard
about the death of Habyarimana and how the genocide was taking place, they had no choice but to get back into the fight. From
that night of April 6, 1994, it took them one hundred days to
achieve victory. It took thirty days to get to Rukumbeli as they
were rescuing people and recruiting young men for battle. My
older brother Vianney was the first of my brothers to join the RPF.

VIANNEY'S STORY

Jean Marie Vianney is the fourth of my parents' eight children
and only two years older than me. He loved to play soccer and do
business with our father, who taught him how to build houses.
After he graduated primary school, he had to find a job, so he
went about four hours away to the city of Kibungo to work with
our uncle who lived there.

When the genocide started in his town, thousands of people
ran to the Catholic church nearby. The priest gave them into the
hands of the killers to destroy them. Very soon, the Hutu began
slaughtering people right in front of Vianney's eyes, so he lay
down as if he was dead. He stayed that way until everyone else
was killed and laid on top of him.

The killers took spears and stabbed them into the piles of bodies to make sure that no one was still alive. Laying at the bottom
of a pile, the spears barely missed him. They would go through
the person on top of him and stop right before they pierced him.

Later that night, the killers came back and threw grenades
into the church to make sure no one survived. The bodies on top

of my brother protected him, so he was unhurt. As far as he knew, he was the only person that survived the attack at the church. He tried all night to get the bodies off him. When he was finally free, Vianney was covered with blood from head to toe.

Then he walked miles and miles, trying to find any other Tutsi that had survived. He didn't know which way to go, but began walking north. Unfortunately, he ran right into a large group of Hutu heading to Tanzania.

The government of Habyalimana had poisoned the minds of both Hutu and Tutsi for years. We were told that the RPF were not human—that they were like animals, which had tails and long ears and ate people. We were told that they killed people in despicable ways. As soon as Fred died, the military of Habyalimana created a song aimed at wiping out any hope in the RPF. They presented the song in the national stadium, gloating of how they had killed the leader of the RPF. It served its purpose of discouraging Tutsi.

The RPF had their own radio station that ran sporadically from the mountains of Birunga. They could not broadcast often, for fear of being caught. Their broadcasts usually lasted only about two hours a day. The radio station was named Muhabura after one of the highest mountains in Rwanda in the Birunga mountain range.

They played many songs written to explain who they were and what their mission was. It was from that radio station that many Rwandans learned that the aim of the RPF was to unite all Rwandans. Most Hutu did not believe what they heard, but Tutsis gained hope. There was one particular song, "Umunezero," by a singer named Kayirebwa Cecile that was a beautiful beacon of hope to many of us. She said that her song was created from joy. I remember hiding in the bushes listening with wonder.

Because of the hate propaganda on the national radio station, many Hutu now fled for their lives. They truly feared the RPF as nonhuman ravenous animals. There was a large group of Hutu moving northeast into Tanzania. It was that group that Vianney ran into.

There was an older gentleman among them that took Vianney under his wing by pretending he was with him. He was a friend of our uncle. Vianney traveled with the group all the way to the border of Tanzania. There they could not decide what to do with him. They said he did not look like one of them; he looked too much like a Tutsi. They debated for some time, and finally they decided to kill him. Aware of their decision, he fled.

As he was fleeing from the group of Hutu, he ran into the RPF. One of the *afande* (RPF commanders) was very curious about him and interviewed him carefully. He wanted to know who his father was. When Vianney told him he was a son of Makombe Andre, the man acted surprised and asked who his mother was. As soon as he said Marie the man seemed amazed. He acted like Joseph in the Bible when he recognized his brothers. He ordered his men to cook meat for him and gave him a bed.

Vianney slept in amazement and wonder, not knowing why he was so blessed by the man. The next day the afande approached Vianney and introduced himself. He said that he was called Mandevu (which means "beards," and he truly did have a long beard). He told Vianney that he was a distant uncle and had left Rwanda thirty years before because of the first genocide.

Vianney then began to train and work with the RPF. He traveled with them, fighting to liberate our tribe. One time, a bomb was thrown into his group, and it fell right in front of him. It formed a large hole in the ground, and he fell into it. He was buried alive, and the rest of his troop thought that he was dead, so they moved on. Soon they saw a gun waving around, sticking up from where Vianney was buried. They rushed in and dug him out.

GREGORY'S STORY

My cousin Gregory was a tall, strong young man of dignity. His parents, my aunt Janet and her husband Atanase, were refugees of the first genocide who had fled to Congo. He was born and raised in the Congo until he decided to come to Rwanda with his mother to visit us for the first time in the 1990s. His mom left him in Rwanda because he liked it there and was old enough to do some business. Soon he met friends who led him to the Lord, and he became a true Jesus follower. He was very disciplined and educated in religious ways. He became a church planter in the Eastern Province of Rwanda, but his Hutu boss found him enjoying more favor with God and became jealous of him.

At that time it was hard to cross the borders of Rwanda because the RPF was already fighting against the Hutu regime. As soon as he learned that there was no chance for him to succeed in ministry because of his tribe, he decided to join the RPF. On his way, he was put in prison for a long time when the government discovered his intentions. Eventually he was released and came back home to see us again.

He was a man of visions and dreams, courageous and full of hope. He always sang hymns about heaven, and the sound of his voice is always in my heart, especially his favorite song that told us to look back and ask yourself if your will reach heaven.

He never gave up his courage. He saw how his people were treated and knew it wasn't right, so he made another way to get to the RPF. After he connected with them, he was trained well and was accepted as part of the Inkotanyi (another name for the RPF that means "warriors"). It was his dream to one day see his nation in freedom and his parents returned to their homeland. He longed for this more than anything else in this world and was willing to give his life to make it happen.

After my brothers, he was the man I wanted to see most. He had so much hope in him that I needed, but I never knew where he got it or how to get it myself. I just wished to be like him.

In the first week of May, Gregory and Vianney led a team into our village. They knew the place well, so they brought a company of a few soldiers to search for any survivors. The first time they tried to come, they were in a convoy, but they had complications with the vehicle and had to turn back. We had watched the Interahamwe escaping, and when we noticed that they no longer fled, we knew that the RPF must be close. We awaited their arrival with much peace and hope.

That evening, we sent some of our young men, including Ephrem, to go to the Interhamwe camp to see if it had been occupied by the RPF. When they arrived, they discovered that the RPF were, in fact, there, and they stayed with them. Ephrem met Gregory and Vianney in the camp and told them of our group. Because it was late in the evening, they decided to come for us the next day.

The next morning, a few of us gathered together and waited for our spies to return, but no one showed up until midday. It was hard to find all of us in one place because we were still in hiding. The RPF came on foot, with Vianney leading the team. Because he was from our village and would be recognized by us, he was put in front of the group marching into our area. He moved forward announcing his name and calling people out of hiding in the marshes.

Another team was sent to the area where we were hiding. They were spotted along the way, and those who saw them ran to us to announce their arrival. Most of us rushed to meet them, but a small group doubted. We met them on the road, where they announced who they were and said that they were there to rescue us. We had wondered what they looked like. We had heard stories about them on the radio, but we could not imagine them. My whole life, the only soldiers we had ever seen were part of the national army that came to beat and kill us. To us, a uniform evoked fear and dread.

We all went to see what good soldiers who actually cared about us must look like. When we saw them, they appeared to be a tough but broken group of men. They were kind to us, but they seemed so hardened. Looking back now, I can imagine what those soldiers must have been through. They had advanced, searching for survivors, searching for their own people. Again and again, they were disappointed, as they found their own families and friends slaughtered. We witnessed so much death in our area, but surely they had seen much more. They must have been numb, having exhausted every bit of emotion left within them.

Our friend Rutagengwa, Shyaka, and I did not trust them, and we withdrew from the crowd to discuss our fears. We did not think that they looked like us and thought it might be a trick of Habyarimana's soldiers to wipe us out completely. The RPF soldiers traveled along the road, carrying the injured. We followed them about a kilometer away, along the edge of the lake. We thought that if they took our people to the east, we could trust that they were RPF; if they took them to the west, we would know we were betrayed.

As we traveled through Rukumbeli and got close to where the open-air market used to be, we saw where the RPF was camping. From a distance, we recognized a different kind of military in the camp.

That is when we finally took hope; we were overwhelmed with the knowledge that they really were coming to our rescue, and our answer had finally come. We knew joy in that time more than we ever had. We jumped and danced, rejoicing the whole way, as we ran to them. We could not believe it was true; the RPF really did exist. They were not cockroaches and beasts, as we had been told, but they were our heroes, our deliverers.

As we joined them in the camp, we saw all of the other survivors that we had separated ourselves from. That is when we saw trucks full of soldiers singing songs of victory. As they attacked, they sang songs of hope and assured victory to keep up their morale and unify themselves. It was then that we got a true picture of who the RPF were. I can still remember the songs they sang. All our lives we feared that we would be killed. Seeing our deliverance brought freedom like we had never known before. One song they used to sing was this:

> RPF tutasonga (songa mbere)
> Vita bado ijyaisha kwenye inchi yetu.
> Hatuta toka kwa mobailo hadi
> Tutawaondowa wale wabaya wote.

In English, that means:

> RPF, we will advance (move forward)
> Soon the war will be over in our nation.
> We will never stop marching,
> Until we remove all the evil people.

We stayed in the camp as long as my brothers were part of the RPF and continued to help rescue the rest of the nation. I wanted to join the army so badly. I was never allowed to join those that were fighting because they said I was too young. I had to stay in the camp with the women and elderly, helping to find and prepare any food that we could.

As I stayed in the camp with the RPF, I got a different picture of Rwanda. I heard people speaking of hope for a unified nation. It was so different from the hate propaganda that I had heard for so long. I had never heard people speaking with optimism of the future of my country. I expected the RPF to help me get revenge on those that had ruined my life, but I was shocked that they spoke of peace and unity. I had never understood or thought of the concept of unity or harmony before.

There was another song I heard them singing that seemed like a message of life to me:

> Amuka kadogo (songa)
> nawe muzee
> Songa utsimbure
> icyo gitugu
> Ubabwire y'uko

Urwanda
arurw'imbaga
y'inyabutatu
ya Gihanga.
Insinzi bana B'urwanda insinzi
Ge ndayireba insinzi
Mubice byose insinzi

Here is its translation:

Get up, young one (move)
and you, old one.
Go and move
that dictatorship.
Tell them that
Rwanda
belongs to the family
of the three
born of Gihanga.
Victory, Children of Rwanda, Victory!
I see it, victory,
On all sides, victory!

I didn't know how anyone could think of unity so soon, but I didn't realize that they had thought of it all along. I was told in the camp that Paul Kagame had made a rule that, if anyone killed a civilian, he should be killed as well. I thought I would hate him forever because of that rule and no one would agree with him. The need for revenge pumped through my veins, and I hated Kagame for speaking of peace and denying me what I thought I deserved.

Now I can look back and appreciate the rule. It was what was needed. If I had enacted my revenge, it might have destroyed me. Surely I was not the only one who wanted to hurt the Hutu as they had hurt us and more. If we had not been prevented from doing so, Rwanda would surely be a different place today.

I stayed in the camp with my uncle Russ and worked for him in his business. He made me feel like we were both owners of the company. He set up a makeshift bar in one of the houses in the camp. While he and his wife manned it, I was in the bush secretly making the local beer, called *waragi*. This beer was illegal and very dangerous, which is why I had to hide in the bush to brew it.

He spent his time drinking and selling beer with his wife, keeping the money and having fun. I was always drinking and eating very little, until the beer seemed to take over my blood, and I began to suffer different kinds of sicknesses. With no doctor to treat me, I suffered more and more. I wondered if there could be any hope for me, living that kind of life with nobody to care for me. Even as I was lost in despair, God had a plan for my life.

ANOTHER SURPRISE

Jeanne d'Arc Mukashyaka was the third child and my elder sister, who helped my mom to raise her younger siblings, including me. Although she grew up happy with many girls in our community, because she was the only older girl in our family, she worked so hard. She was always decorating our house, painting, and making mats with other girls in our village. She was the most beautiful girl in her school, and the boys loved her so much. It was for that reason one of the Hutu boys kidnapped her in the first weeks of the genocide to marry her someday. However, his fellow Hutu would not let him. He had a strong family that had influence in the government, so they were respected. Otherwise he was at risk hiding a Tutsi girl.

One day she heard them saying that they were about to take her away and kill her because they knew her brother Vianney was fighting against them and they were losing the battle. As soon as she learned that, she escaped and stayed in the bush for some-time, not knowing what was going on.

After walking aimlessly, she heard the sound of people talking and thought it would be a good idea to come closer and see what it was. It was the middle of July when she showed up in the camp. People came to me and told me that my sister was still alive and was among us. What a blessing to have her back!

She joined us in the camp, and the next year, we had our own place to stay together. She took care of me until she wasn't able to help me anymore. I was a drunken young man, who cared about nothing in life since we lost our parents. I didn't value anything or anybody around me.

Once a year, one of our brothers would come and visit with us and make sure we were doing well. I wasn't, but they never knew it. Inside of me was emptiness, fear, and hopelessness—so much that I thought death was better than life. I also thought I was dead.

Even though I could remember the whole event, there was great confusion about how around 49,000 had died and only three hundred of us were still alive in that small town (the number of Tutsi in Rukumbeli before the war is not sure. It was between fifty thousand and eighty thousand and the number of survivors is between three hundred and seven hundred). It seemed impossible that I could be among the three hundred survivors.

There was nothing special about me. I didn't think I was good enough to survive. If there was a God, surely he would not have chosen me to live, when there were others that were more worthy of survival. I was the kid that my family and neighbors taunted with stupid names. I was haunted with the thought that there were others that should have lived instead of me.

CHAPTER 4
AFTER THE GENOCIDE

FACING THE UNSPEAKABLE

In this very small country, we saw things that no one can describe in a book—some of the worst the world has ever seen. People were killed in hideous ways. It became the custom of the Hutu extremists to torture families in a way that produced pain that was both physical and psychological. When a family was found together, they would kill the children first and make the parents watch because the parents were able to comprehend more and thus suffered more. The children's arms or legs were cut off first, and then their throats were slit. Often the killers would save the most humiliating act for last: just before a child died, they would cut off their genitalia and taunt the parents with it as a sign that there would be no more reproduction of the Tutsi, that the Hutu would achieve total victory. Some Tutsi were burned in their houses, tortured, and cut into pieces. My mother was one of those who had her legs and arms cut off and her throat slit before she was left to die. They also killed my baby brother, whom my mother carried on her back, though I don't know how. She spent a lot of time in agony before she died.

When I told people my story, for many years I left out how my mother had died because I was not able to talk about it. I pretended that I never knew what happened to her, and I wouldn't answer any questions about it. It was too painful to admit to myself what had happened. She was my mother, the biggest love I knew was for her, and I had left her.

However, as years passed, I began to open up to people. When they asked me if I witnessed the death of my mother, it felt like a knife was plunged into my stomach. I had not witnessed it, but I felt I should have. I was haunted with the conviction that I should not have left her and should have been there with her. The pain was so deep because the thing that was the most precious to me had not only been taken away, but she had to die in such a horrific way. How could I make sense of life or hope for any good when my beautiful mother died slowly and in agony with her arms and legs cut off and her baby ripped from her grasp?

In the early years after the genocide, I could not deal with the issue. I even made light of the situation, saying that I had told her to run and she should have listened to me. I had to keep the situation far from my heart.

Finally, I had to face people's questions and interviews about the genocide. People need to know the whole story, and they have to know life as we know it. I had to tell what happened to my mother. I had to get it out. I had to finally allow myself to grieve for her. When I did, it was painful. The hurt seemed to consume me, but the Great Comforter was with me and helped me to finally heal.

MISPLACED HOPE

The horror that occurred in Rwanda was not the first time this earth has seen such atrocities, and it was not the last. Murder was born in the second generation from Adam. It did not take long for nations to rise against others for the sake of power, greed, and hatred.

Habyalimana and certain leaders in the French government were bonded in their corruption and greed. They were selfish and power-hungry. Satan used their common hatred for our tribe to do horrible things. They made a plan to destroy the Tutsi tribe completely. Many, many Hutu were brainwashed to hate the Tutsis already, and then they were trained to kill them in gruesome ways. While the world was led to believe that the reports of genocide were exaggerated, innocent men, women, and children were mutilated for sport.

They had power and influence and were able to fool many other nations for too long. We live in a fallen world, and our countries are led by fallen people. The temptations of this world and upside-down priorities drive men. If national leaders do not know the truth, they cannot guide their countries by it. Many politicians try to hide their own evil deeds by pointing accusing fingers at their opponents. That is the way this world has taught us to defend ourselves. For those that fear the Lord and follow his ways, He is their defense.

While Rwanda was facing this tragedy, many nations were watching but did nothing about it because the devil is the ruler of this world. Our minds have been corrupted by the traditions and cultures of this world that created a worldview ultimately unbiblical. As Interahamwe drank and shouted chants of Hutu power, UN soldiers walked away from a Tutsi–safe zone that they had been guarding. Without hesitation, the Interahamwe rushed in and slaughtered the thousands inside while the UN soldiers simply drove away.

Before the genocide occurred, several nations were warned. In-depth details of the plan were sent out with hope from a repentant Hutu leader, but they were ignored.

However, my hope is not in nations. My hope is in the Lord, the Maker of heaven and earth.

When ancient Israel learned that surrounding nations were going to attack them, the good kings of Israel went to inquire of the Lord. Many times God gave them strategies that saved their nation. The wisdom of the Lord is perfection, while the wisdom of the wisest man is foolishness to God. A nation whose leaders fear the Lord has true hope. Our hope will never come from the wisdom of men.

Rwanda and its people were forsaken by other nations. While some nations were involved in the planning and carrying out of mass murder, all other nations sat back and watched it happen. The rest of the world did nothing, while a million lives were lost. No one seemed to care about Tutsi or Hutu lives as long as none of their own citizens were hurt. If it weren't for foreigners present in Rwanda, many nations might not have been concerned at all. Other African presidents had been so corrupted by the hunger for power that they were too focused on their own prosperity to do anything. Even though UN soldiers were in place in Rwanda, many were ordered by their sending countries to take no part in the intervention of mass murder and were even ordered to not carry Rwandan citizens in their vehicles.

The worries and cares of this world can prevent us from impacting it for the sake of Christ. We teach our children to stand up for the defenseless but do not model it in our own lives. It is often not modeled internationally unless there is something to be gained by one country defending another. James 1:27 says that true religion is to look after widows and orphans. This is a call to care for those who are defenseless. If we stood up sooner, this world would see a lot fewer widows and orphans.

The genocide in Rwanda was not planned overnight, nor was it prepared for overnight. It was not a secret. Many other nations were aware of the situation, but they did nothing to prevent it or even to stop it once it began.

Africa needs to raise up good leaders who are not just educated in European or American universities. They should be people who have proven their love for their own nations, who are willing to sacrifice their own blood for others, instead of sacrificing the whole nation for the advancement of those in power. If you don't love your own nation and are not willing to fight for it, how can you expect anyone else to?

We need more heroes who stand for something real without fear. The world loves to remember heroes, but no one wants to be one. We applaud those who stand up against opposition for what is right, but most of us are afraid to make that stand in our own lives.

Beware of leaders who promise miracles by their own power. They are like the pharaoh of Egypt, whom the King of Assyria called a "splintered reed of a staff, which pierces a man's hand and wounds him if he leans on it" (2 Kings 18:21, NIV). You can vote for a man who puts his trust in Jesus—the highest, most powerful name—because from the beginning, this is the only name that had victory and has never failed anyone who trusted in Him. Surely the King of Assyria was right when he discredited the pharaoh of Egypt to Hezekiah, even though he said it as a ploy to destroy his confidence. The Lord was his only hope and is our only hope today.

This is how it is with kings of the earth. Many care too much about their own power or revenge until they themselves become victims of war. Politicians stand before men trying to gain their votes, sounding like gods. They promise miracles of their own doing. They promise to be the change nations are looking for. But what did they change before they decided to run for office? What difference have they made? How have they shown their love for their nation before being elected? Are we supposed to believe that as soon as they take office, we will see what they care about? We need to open our eyes in this struggling world.

There has never been and will never be a faithful king like Jesus Christ. For that reason, the most successful leaders are the ones that trust in Him. In Africa, there have been countless national leaders that have trusted in other gods or trusted in their own strength and wreaked destruction over the nations they led. We have seen dictators and evil men all but destroy our lands.

Better is a dog hit by a car on the road than those men and those that put their trust in them.

I remember in the days of our slaughter, watching airplanes fly freely over our heads, wondering how so many other people could just continue life as normal all around us, not caring about the depravity engulfing us. The Western mind-set has been that Africans are having conflicts and some kind of civil wars between themselves all the time, so they should be left alone. Surely the worst enemy of Africa is Africans themselves. Other nations watched the genocide happen, but none came to our aid. They sat back and argued about what to do until the RPF gained control and stopped the killings alone.

In three months, over a million people lost their lives. Afterward, we had representatives from many nations coming to Rwanda to defend their reputations with a lot of lies, claiming that they hadn't known. The United Nations was there to keep peace, but there was no peace for them to keep, and they surely didn't bring peace! Some of the UN soldiers would take in Tutsi, telling them that they would help them, but then they would hand them over to the Interhamwe.

Even if the rest of the world sat back and watched our horror, they are not to blame. Our solution must come from within. The kingdoms of this world must be focused on the kingdom of God if real change is to come.

The head of the UN, along with other national leaders, denied that what happened in Rwanda was genocide. They claimed that it was a civil war. When the secretary general of the UN came to Rwanda to investigate, he was not received well by Rwandans. I was there watching and hearing the news of politicians arguing and playing games, while civilians perished. We can put our trust in politicians and sing their praises, but someday they may turn out to be our killers.

WORSHIPING MEN AS GODS

In the 1980s, when I was growing up, we were taught to worship our president, who had been involved in killing thousands of Tutsi—including my grandparents—in 1959. Our leaders called it Revolution Hutu, where they defeated their enemy (the Tutsi). Habyalimana Juvenal was a leader in the army. He killed the man who was president in the seventies and took his place. He was a dictator and brainwashed people to convince them that he was their father.

Songs were written for him; dancers were chosen in every region of the country to perform for Habyalimana Juvenal, the father of the whole nation. He called himself the unbeatable or undefeated one. Every year, we celebrated him with dances and songs.

We were brainwashed and blinded about this evil man, who was used by the devil all those years. Like any other president who wants to gain favor from people, he always promised miracles by his own power but died before he could accomplish any of them. He wasn't even able to save himself from dying, but people still believed in him. Even I was impressed with his power. The whole time he was president, he acted like he was in support of a united Rwanda, but all the time, he was plotting the next genocide and was secretly killing Tutsi and Hutu that tried to speak out or rise up against him.

Around 1990, I began to understand the truth of what had been happening in my country. It was then that the RPF first attacked. This emboldened many to speak out, who had been silent for so many years.

After the genocide, I hated anything about leadership because all I could see was their potential to hurt. I thought that all leaders were bent on ruling people and controlling them. I wondered what evil was hidden in their hearts. I didn't care about anything and separated myself from politics completely, even refusing to vote. But praise God, who can heal our brains and renew them! I never thought I could support any president or anyone in government. It took me a very long time to believe that God could find faithful people to lead nations.

By July 1994, the RPF had taken control of every province in Rwanda. Most of the national army and Interhamwe were defeated and forced out of the country. The RPF then concentrated on finding and stopping the small groups that were hidden within Rwanda. Bizimungu Pastor became president immediately following the fighting. He was a Hutu politician who had supported the RPF, and he was chosen to be president by the newly formed government. However, terrorist attacks continued for a decade more. Hutu power groups bombed buses, tourist places, and Tutsi in villages, trying to regain power. Even in 2012, there were grenade attacks with political motivation in public places in Rwanda.

LIFE WITHOUT PURPOSE

The way the genocide affected me was unique. Like everyone else around, I chose to adopt any life that was available. The life I fell into was one of drunkenness. I made local beer day and night. I drank too much and had no control because I wanted to forget. I tried so hard to kill the memories in my brain, that I damaged so much more with my ruinous drinking.

Because I was always drunk, day and night lost their meaning. I would make beer until night and then go to the bar and drink with whoever was there. I only slept if I passed out or if there was no one else around to drink with. I worked through the night and the next morning went on drinking. That was my life. All I did was make beer and drink.

My heart was blind. I was living life with no goals, no purpose or vision. People called my name, and I thought it was a dream. I couldn't comprehend reality. Life was so hard in Rwanda, especially for children my age that were orphaned with no one to parent them. I tried to pretend to be like everyone else.

Many, like my brothers, had purpose. They were soldiers, and even though they witnessed the same horrors that I did, they were able to channel their grief and anger into fighting.

I was lost. My life as I knew it was gone. I no longer had parents. I didn't have chores. I didn't have school. I had no purpose and felt useless. I had no reason to get up in the morning. I thought I had nothing to live for, so I threw my life away.

The way I wanted to live was the way most teenagers would like to live when they are not in Christ. I just wanted to look like a big man who goes to drink in a bar the whole night, dancing and getting drunk. I didn't see hope for any kind of future for myself, so I destroyed my own life slowly.

People wanted me to go to school, but since they had no authority over me, they couldn't do anything about it. I just heard them talking to each other. My mind changed about education. I no longer believed that it was a good thing. Those in my village that were the most educated were the most hunted. Their education became their downfall.

After some time, and because of much pressure, I began to think that maybe there was hope for me in education. I tried a few days, but I couldn't do it. My mind was not able to focus on anything. I quit and went back to drinking. It wasn't easy knowing that among my brothers, I was the only one who had a chance to go to school and I couldn't do it. They all tried to help me go back. For that reason, I felt like I was forced to go back to school. I went back, even though I didn't think I could, and I failed again and again.

A NEW FAMILY

By July, the survivors of Rukumbeli had set up a kind of refugee community and lived together in the houses that surrounded the open-air market. The Rwandans who had fled to Burundi as refugees of the 1959 genocide began to return home. My hometown was close, so many came to settle there. They traveled very far in the back of cargo trucks and arrived covered in dust. After they were dropped off in the center of the village, they began asking around to learn whether any of their relatives had survived.

All of these families looked different than us. They had lives, and their minds were focused. I didn't care about those coming back into the country. I didn't think I needed anyone.

I heard about a family in the crowd that mentioned the name of my mother. I ran around asking who they were, and a friend told me a name that sounded familiar because my mom used to mention it once in a while. Elevanie was her name, and her husband and children were with her. I learned that she was my mom's sister.

Soon after they settled, I went to see them with one of the elders in town who had known them thirty years earlier. We knew that they had settled in our area, but we did not know which house was theirs. When we passed by the house, the elder stopped his bicycle abruptly. I asked him what had happened.

"That voice," he replied. He had heard Elevanie talking.

Very quickly we rushed through the fence and knocked on the door. She came out and looked at us with wonder in her eyes. The elder introduced himself and told her that he was close to the family of Makombe.

Without hesitation and with her hands gripping his shoulders, she asked, "Tell me now, is there anyone who survived in my sister's family?" She had tears in her eyes, not able to believe such a miracle was possible.

The elder turned around and pointed a finger at me. "Here is your nephew," he informed her.

I can't explain her emotions at that moment, but she grabbed me and wrapped her arms around me, dropping tears on my shoulders. I had very few emotions left in me, after what I had been through, but at that moment I felt the first stirrings in my heart since I felt it had died.

When my mother was frightened or moved emotionally, she used to say the name of her father, Joas, in exclamation. This woman Elevanie did the same thing. It was a sign to me that she truly was my mother's sister.

It felt so good to have another loving mother who would care about how I was doing. After a long time crying and sobbing, she introduced me to her children, who stood there amazed to see their new cousin. They didn't expect to see any survivors in their family. There were no signs of hope in our village. It was so destroyed that most of the houses had been burned or torn down.

We sat down for a while, and they began to ask questions about how we survived the terror that overtook our village. Because Elevanie had been away for such a long time without a way of communication, her family knew little of ours. They wanted to know how many kids were in my father's house. When I told them eight, they seemed full of sorrow and asked me if I was the only one left out of all the children.

I told them that I was not the only one, that my three older brothers were soldiers, and that I lived with my older sister. Joy flooded back into their hearts with the good news that there was even more of their family alive. I could not give them hope about my mother, so I carefully tried not to say anything about her. They understood the reason I had not mentioned her and did not ask me about her or my father.

My sister and I visited them often. My aunt had one son who was in the RPF. She lived in the village with four of her daughters, two grandchildren, and her husband Dismas. She told me about three other daughters that she had, who were older and not with her then. From that time on, they became my new family.

For us, life was only what we could see at the present time. The children of my aunt went to school with much confidence. When I looked at them, I didn't understand why they were working hard for things that were not beneficial, like school.

SCHOOL DAZE

I went to primary school a few times, and there was a big boy who tormented me in class. He used to push me off my chair, but I never complained because I didn't care what happened to me. I remembered who I used to be before the genocide and just wanted to think that it was a dream.

The teachers tried to teach the whole class as if I was one of them. They tested us more often, but I don't remember anything that I was able to put on paper. Every semester, we had exams; and most of the time, I was late or absent in class because my concept of time was different from anyone else. I slept whenever I was very tired, no matter what time it was. When I woke up in the afternoon, I had to go to school and would meet other kids coming home. I told myself that it must have been some kind of holiday. Then I went home for a week or so, while others did their national testing.

I couldn't comprehend reality and didn't understand that I was not on the same schedule as everyone else. Somehow I got lost and could not remember about school. That is when I had to move from Kibungo to Kigali for health issues. I was drinking too much and eating too little, and my body began to give out.

LIFE IN KIGALI

About a year after the genocide, I was living with my sister in Kibungo. One day I fainted, and she rushed me in the bus to Kigali, where we found a hospital. I was able to stay with some relatives who lived there, which helped keep me away from alcohol for some time. I then began to gain some understanding through the people that I lived with.

One of my cousins who had survived in the area called Ruhanga in Kigali town, was there: Shyaka Theoneste. Like me, he was angry about what had happened to him and wanted to give up on life. His parents were killed, along with all seven of his siblings. He was the only survivor in his family. He was older than me, and he took care of me and my aunt's family as he was making some money in small businesses there. Some nights I went to the bar with him and drank with some of his other friends that were survivors. I lived there with my cousin for between two and three years.

Every year in April was very hard for all of us as it meant the national week of mourning is approaching. The radio and TV played memorial songs, and we drank and shared testimonies. We cried and comforted each other. However, sometimes we were violent, beating everyone we met day and night until April passed.

That is when I met Aunt Janete, the oldest among my mother's siblings. She was one of the refugees of the 1959 genocide who had fled to Congo. She had fled with her husband Atanase. All three of their sons were in the army, helping the nation to recover. My cousin Gregory, whom I loved so much, was one of them. When I met them, they lived with their three daughters. None of them had jobs or any other resources, but I always saw the hand of God leading them through all of their crises and providing for them.

Joining that family was not easy for me, even though they were my relatives. We never felt right together because we had different stories. They could never understand what I was going through and how I felt. My heart needed somebody who felt the same way I did.

That is why I spent most of my time with my cousin Shyaka Theoneste and his other survivor friends. When they told stories, I felt like I was not alone in my struggle. They seemed like brothers to me.

Because it was expected, I had to spend some time with Aunt Janete and her family, especially her husband Atanase. I was more comfortable with him. He used to tell me stories of my ancestry, which helped me understand who I really was.

Even though I was supposed to stay with my aunt's family, my pride wouldn't let me. I wanted to look older than I was and be somebody I wasn't. This attitude got me in trouble. Friends continued to encourage me to do wrong, and I easily followed them. I was fifteen years old, but I tried to act like I was twenty-five.

Part of the problem was the constant reminder of my mother. Jeanette looked almost exactly like her. When I looked at her, I couldn't block out the memory of what had happened to my mom. So I stayed with other young men and did what they did.

CHAPTER 5
BACK TO SCHOOL

REPEATING PRIMARY CLASSES

In 1995, I went back to try primary school in a small town called Ruhanga, right outside of Kigali town. This time I was really trying to understand why we needed to go to school and learn. My life was changing, and my vision began to grow larger. I began to have some hope for my future and think that I could make something of my life. There was still a lot of work that needed to be done, however. Something was still missing, and I had no idea what it was.

After I had struggled so much in school after the war, I decided to go back to primary five, even though I had passed it before the war in Rukumberi. My brain was so confused; it was as if I had forgotten what I had once known. I really wanted to pass my schooling, so I thought that it was good to go back as far as I needed to and do as much as my traumatized brain could handle. This time I wanted to get somewhere.

A big problem that Africa is facing right now is that kids go to school without proper nutrition, so they are not really able to learn well. As they overtax their undernourished brains, it wears out their bodies. That was a big problem of mine at that time. I was really trying to succeed, but I struggled so much. I studied day and night, trying to make up for the fact that my brain was still not functioning normally. There was hardly ever nutritious food available and never enough of what I could find. I got weaker and weaker, sicker and sicker. Most of the time, I went to bed hungry and had to get up early in the morning to get ready for school.

READY TO QUIT SCHOOL AND WORK

After I passed primary five, I tried to pass primary six, but I failed the national test that would allow me to go to secondary school. I remember that I had to walk about two hours to get to the district office to check on my test results. When I got there, many other students were so happy that they had passed, and they expected me to pass too. Unfortunately, my scores were just below the cut-off line. I gave up at that point and was no longer willing to go to school.

It was the summer of 1997 when I gave up on school. I decided to go to Kigali town where my brothers, Ephrem and Shyaka, had started a barber shop so that I could work for them to make a living. Ephrem had named the salon "Copernic" after his favorite scientist. It was there for almost ten years.

One afternoon in July, I took the bus to Kigali. When my brothers saw me, they were relieved because they needed someone to stay in the shop to manage the business. There I was, with a few guys from Ruhanga. My brothers hired them because they were hometown boys and wanted to help them also. At that time, my brother Shyaka was still serving in the armed forces. Ephrem was out of the military, attending secondary school near the business, so he kept an eye on me in case I got into trouble. He collected the money every evening to save it in a safe place. The business did not do well with Ephrem and me running it.

All during the summer break, I was convinced that I was not going back to school. All my brothers wanted me to go back though. Shyaka took me back, and I obeyed him. I went to primary school again in a town called Gikondo, which was about a forty-five-minute walk from where I lived. I wanted to go to secondary school so badly, I tried primary six again. I was able to be more independent in this school and didn't feel like it was as torturous as Ruhanga.

I worked every evening and made enough money for the bus or to eat in a restaurant. I felt proud of myself. I made friends at school, and joy came back into my life. I could see some hope, but I was still not sure if I would be able to pass the test at the end of the year.

BEST SCHOOL IN THE COUNTRY

One time I went to a festival at one of the well-equipped secondary schools (high schools), called Saint Andre. That was the best school I had ever seen in my life.

I remember praying a short prayer asking God to do a miracle and bring me there. At the end of my year at Gikondo, my leaders at school were so proud of me and hoped that I would graduate. I went to the national exams with fear and trembling, but I made it with a good score that allowed me to go to Saint Andre secondary school. When I saw my scores, I doubted that they were mine and thought that they must have belonged to someone else. Walking home was an amazing experience, and it felt like a big promotion in my life.

As soon as the next school year started, I couldn't wait to buy a uniform and pack my bag to go to the highest rated school in the country. As I walked in the gates, the gatekeepers opened the doors for me and welcomed me warmly. I felt like a prince walking on a red carpet. Soon I was given a room that I shared with seven other students. It was the most organized lifestyle that I had ever seen.

They rang the bell early in the mornings for Catholic devotions in the chapel. I attended regularly, even though it was not mandatory. I longed to be with God, even though I didn't fully understand what it meant. It was just something inside of me seeking an answer to all of my questions about life.

Many of the other students had the same feelings as I did about how everything was so new and overwhelming. There were so many rich kids in that school, and they were very smart, which made me feel like a loser. Some were twelve or thirteen years old, and I was eighteen. The young kids did better than me in class, even though I was much older.

KARATE—MY PASSPORT TO SUCCESS AND RESPECT

Every Wednesday, it was recommended that every student got involved in some kind of sport or fun activity. I tried many of them but liked soccer. I played soccer for almost a year until my equipment needed to be replaced. I could not afford to buy more, so I quit. Soon a friend invited me to go with him to watch the students studying karate. We both liked it but feared that we would get injured. As we continued to visit, we decided to give it a try.

My friend knew a few moves, and he started to prepare me. As a loser, everything my hand found to do I did it with all my strength because I wanted to prove myself. After two weeks, I heard that the karate class was having a day of testing. Those who passed got a belt or a promotion to a higher belt. I ran quickly and stepped in line for the testing. I had never taken a class before and hadn't officially learned any moves, but I was sure that I could learn as I went and pass. I never liked theory, but I loved the practical application of things.

When the teacher saw me, he was amazed at how I could follow right along with the other students and even do the moves better than the ones that had been trained. That was my first day in karate. Everything I learned was what I had watched from a distance or the few basic moves that my friend had taught me. After I had failed at so many things, I couldn't believe that I was actually being accepted and achieving something.

At the end of the day, when the teacher was handing out belts, he gave me an orange belt. That was the highest possible belt that we could receive in our category. Orange was level three, and many of the more experienced guys were given yellow, which was level two. Many of them were angry and jealous of me, so they planned to challenge me the next day. Somehow I was so happy to be succeeding at something that I didn't care if I made enemies doing it.

The whole school heard the news that I had received an orange belt, and many of the other students began to respect me in a way that they had not before. However, my biggest challenge was that many thought that I had not earned it, so I had to make sure I could defend it.

Getting that orange belt was probably the first thing I ever did in my life that gained me any kind of recognition. I was happier than ever just to be someone. I had felt so discouraged most of my life because of the names my father and others had called me. Then the genocide had taken away any hope I had of even being normal again. I feared to be injured in karate though, because some of the more experienced students were out to get me. I was a nobody who had come out of nowhere and made them look bad.

The very next day, I was invited to practice, but the teacher was not there. The most advanced student with an orange belt led the practice. As soon as I entered the training room, everybody's eyes were on me. They knew of the plot to shame me. I immediately began trying to think of a way to get out of the room. I knew something was going on, so I was careful in what I did. Soon the leaders asked me to spar with another student who looked angry. He was a yellow belt, and I knew that he was angry with me for passing him so quickly. This guy was short but thick and had trained for a long time.

After greeting each other in the traditional manner for karate, we began. I knew that this match was not for exercise or practice. They meant to put me in my place, and I was afraid.

As soon we started, he punched me square in the chest, and the punch took my breath away for a few minutes. I felt I not only had to defend myself from bodily harm, but I had to defend the new honor that had been given to me. I psyched myself up to not give up but stay in the match.

He knew that I was a new student, but he didn't know that I was actually pretty talented. Usually I could imagine things and put them into action very fast, and every move he made was copied in my mind.

The next time he attacked me, I lifted my leg and kicked him under his chin in anger. He lost control and blood came out of his mouth and nose. He went outside and never came back.

When the rest of them saw that the game changed, I became more confident. I started to pretend that I knew much more about karate than I really did, and I started training day and night, because I knew that I would be challenged again.

Soon I joined the Tigers Club, a famous karate club in Rwanda. Because during school breaks I lived with my brother in the RPF headquarters, I also joined their karate club. They worked so hard and never took breaks. It was just their job to know how to fight. I stayed in their headquarters, and they would wake me up early in the morning at 5:00 a.m. for practice. In the evenings, I went to the Tigers Club.

Soon many soldiers hated me because I was so good at what I learned. I was younger than most of them, and my body was simply more flexible. Their trainer always set me up to fight each one of them, one after another, without a break. I did it though and succeeded. I was so elated by the idea of finally excelling at something, that I had no thought of humility. I became cocky, which made me even more enemies.

One of the teachers there was an older soldier that hated me, and everyone knew it. He approached me with intentions to injure me. He was a black belt, puffed up with pride and lorded it over those who were under him.

Many times in life, people feel like they have to put others down to build themselves up. It is a ploy of Satan that too many of us fall victim to.

This time I fell into the trap. The older soldier hated green belts (which I was at the time). He called me forward to make an example of me.

As I was standing there listening to him talk, I got distracted. He got down and kicked my legs out from under me, and the next thing I knew I was down on the hard floor. I fell on my back and seriously injured it. I stayed down for a while, and then I got up and went home. Because I had landed on my back, I was injured and struggled with severe back pain for a long time.

I didn't have insurance or money to go to the doctor, so I stayed home for several days until the pain in my back subsided and my strength began to return. My back was seriously injured, but we used to say, "If you don't have what you need, enjoy what you have." So I pushed on, focusing on what I did have before me. I continued karate and worked very hard to make sure that one day I could dish out my revenge.

Soon I was chosen to compete in the stadium in Kigali in a national competition. It didn't go very well for me because I made my opponent bleed, which was against the rules. Even if I did not do well in the competition, I knew how good I was becoming. It felt really good to be someone respected in the community. I thought happiness in life came from respect and power. Still empty inside, I mistook my emptiness for a hunger for more power to be able to rule over people. I think that this is a problem that has plagued many rulers across my continent.

I continued my karate training and over time gained more and more respect. I was even chosen to teach karate classes. Although I was finally feeling like I was someone important, still I was not satisfied with my life. I longed for something, but I didn't know what. Nothing seemed to be what I needed. I began to question everything, including my studies.

The first year in Saint Andre secondary school, I was very confused about what I had to study. I didn't know why I had to study. In senior one, I asked my math teacher what the point of algebra was. I was not being rebellious; I really wanted to know if school was something I actually needed to do. I couldn't imagine how life could ever be normal again and what the point was for me to learn anything.

The teacher was so angry with me. She said, "Why do you ask such a question? You are just beginning!"

I wanted to know if this could bring my life back. It looked unnecessary to me, and I didn't want to waste my time. I tried to memorize, but my brain couldn't handle too much. At the end of the year, by chance I was able to pass to senior two. I continued to try to impress the other students by trying to show them that I was someone important. They even voted me to be our class chief. It meant a lot to me that they did that because it meant the students thought they could trust me even though I didn't trust myself. I knew that I was only pretending.

DISCOURAGED AGAIN

From that point, I gained confidence and began to feel great. However, my studies were not going well. Math, physics, chemistry, and so many other subjects were too hard for me to focus my mind on. My brain still did not function like it did before the genocide. I had flashbacks of the killings in my mind when I tried to focus on my work, and then I didn't see the point of learning anything. That year I got kicked out of the school because my scores fell below the cut-off point.

That day I remembered where I had once gone with my friends during lunchtime under the trees behind the school. Young Christians used to meet there to pray and sing hymns. I wanted to go back to see if I could find some hope in life. A few seconds after I got there, two of my friends came to sit with me. One of them asked what my test results were. We all discovered that we had failed our tests and were expelled from the school.

We felt so hopeless until one of the guys comforted us, saying, "Hey, guys, don't worry. *Après les echeques la vie continue.*" It meant, "After failure, life continues." I started to feel like I wasn't alone; I had friends. We decided to go find false papers to be able to continue our school somewhere else. We separated right away on a mission.

I lied to my brothers and told them I passed the exams. The whole summer break I looked for another school. I found one far from town, but I had to go there to cover my shame.

The summer break ended, and all the schools opened. As usual, my brother, Shyaka, with whom I lived, gave me some pocket money. He didn't know that I was going to the other province, Gitarama. He didn't give me enough since Saint Andre was very close. I used to walk there, but now I had to take the bus and ride about four hours.

Just like many guilty people, I ran away in life. I knew that I had not just failed at school, but I had failed my family and friends. I began to feel like I would be better off away, where no one could see me.

CHAPTER 6
SHAME

POOR CHOICES

I wouldn't be able to tell you this part of my life if my shame had not been taken away. My life turned into confusion until I thought it was useless forever, but God had a different view about me. He has always been faithful to me, and I am thankful for the circumstances that brought me to Him.

After I moved to Kigali, I began to conform to the world around me, pretending, but also learning some wisdom from others. Anybody that I met thought of me as normal and even smart because I was a good pretender. About the time I started going to Saint Andre School, I began to feel my age and loved girls like other guys encouraged me to do. I was taught that to become a man was to be with a woman, and I wanted to be a man more than anything. I felt like I was living it up and having fun for the first time in a while.

I made some money every weekend in my brother's barber shop, so I tried to make sure I always looked good, so that girls would notice me. I was still living with pain and shame from my past and thought surely no girl would want to be my girlfriend. I longed to fill the void in me that had not been filled by power, so I tried to fill it with relationships. I worked hard to accomplish my new goal. Soon I had many girls on hold, lying to all of them. Sometimes they knew each other but did not believe each other about me.

I was nineteen years old when I met a girl that I am going to call Joyce. She was very smart, and she was the first girl to ever tell me that she loved me. My heart jumped out of my chest, and I thought I was dreaming.

I met her almost every evening, hoping that someday she would let me sleep with her. Every time we met, my goal was the same. I was so full of lust that it was the only thing in my mind day after day.

I went with my friend to watch adult movies often, which increased my lust even more. Soon I knew that Joyce was very determined to keep herself safe from my intentions. I continued to try somewhere else but kept her close too, in case she changed her mind.

When I think about it today, it saddens me that this might be the case in dating relationships. I hope not all boys think this way, but I am afraid many are just like I was.

One time, I asked my cousin to go tell Joyce that I needed her to visit me, but I told this cousin that I really wanted to have sex. My cousin and I lived in the same house together, and my friends were telling me that I should sleep with her. I told them that, in my family, we respect each other very much. However, they convinced me that it was okay and even better than someone else. So after I talked to her and influenced her with my lust, she agreed, and I had intercourse with her instead of Joyce.

I was so afraid that somehow somebody would find out about this. School was my hiding place, but one day I received a letter from her telling me that she was pregnant. Fear filled my whole being, and I wished to die. The shame was so much that I couldn't have peace. I would have done anything to cover my shame, but there was nothing.

A month passed and then two. She continued to ask me what we were going do, but I was so frustrated and blamed her.

She was confused just like me inside, but I was more to blame because I was the instigator. Soon she told me that her friends had counseled her to abort the baby, but she was so afraid that she would die. She was a Christian in a Pentecostal church, and the shame of a pregnancy would be even greater for her because the choir members that she sang with would recognize her unfaithfulness.

She didn't want to dive into more sin, but she waited for my answer. She invited me for dinner to talk about the issue. This time was not easy for me because I didn't have an answer either. My fear was too consuming. I didn't want to bring shame to my family, but also I didn't want to be a killer.

I remember her asking me a question like, "You know I have friends who support me in abortion, and they told me it's going to be easy. What do you think?"

With my face down, not even looking at her, I questioned, "Did I ever talk to you about a baby, or do you think I wanted a baby?" I was so afraid and tried to put the blame on her, but it was too late to take it back. Even though I was the one that brought this trouble to both of us, I thought it was her fault. I wished she had rejected my advances. I did not want to take responsibility for my actions. I dodged her questions and responded instead with accusations.

She said that she would never give up on her baby. I knew it was a good choice, but still I thought I needed to run away. This was the main reason I ran away, but I also thought it would be good to find another way of success since I was not smart enough for school. My brain was so damaged from alcohol, but I was becoming normal again, except for the stupidity of worldly wisdom. Mostly what I did was my own wrong choices.

I can tell you from experience that the desires of this world are never satisfied by any worldly thing but only by a supernatural God. When I grew up very poor, but never recognized it, I thought that was what life was like. I never knew life beyond mine. When I went to town and began to see how other teens wore good shoes and expensive clothes, lived in beautiful houses, went to night clubs, and had what we called "fun," my heart was burning inside of me and made me feel even more of a failure. Not wanting to be left behind, I tried to follow everybody else.

It took me years to understand that God had a purpose and a specific plan for my life. Instead, I just tried to follow what everyone else was doing. There I was, wandering around without anybody walking with me and nobody to blame. I was making a mess because of the choices I made.

Soon my brothers gathered together to resolve the issues I created. They approached me when I came home to work on the weekend and took me to my cousin, where they had made a small shop for her to sell groceries for a living. They had noticed her belly growing bigger and asked what was going on. She told them the truth, the whole truth.

We sat down together with her, but my mind was so deceitful. I sat there emotionless, hiding my guilt, knowing what was about to happen. One of them asked me quietly, as everybody else was talking about other business, as if it was not a big deal, "Theo, can you please tell us what you did? Are you part of her pregnancy?"

I told them that I was not a part of it, and I didn't know how it could have happened. I remember that it was in the early months of the year 2000. I think I wounded her immensely at that time. I denied her, right to her face.

For a long time, she kept my betrayal in her mind and could not forgive me for all of the wrong I had done to her. It was like I was in a prison of shame. I could not get free of it. She held onto her anger toward me. Because she did not forgive me, it was as if I was bound by her unforgiveness. I was told that she gave birth in July, but I had nothing to do with her or the baby.

STRANGE NEW SCHOOL

In September of 2000, the school year began. I took the bus and didn't tell anyone, except for those who went with me and very close friends. After the long bus ride, we arrived at Ecole Secondaire de Kigoma (ESEKI). It was newly built, but it was small, and there were a lot of students—a lot of weird students. Many of them went to bars at night, were involved in sexual relationships, took drugs, and did many other destructive things. It was so different from Saint Andre.

I went there and was not welcomed by anyone, except for some other students who showed me where the dorms were. I went and looked for my bed, but there was no mattress and no bed sheet. Fortunately, one guy saw me looking lost, and he told me that I could sleep in his bed. His bed was a thin mattress on the floor in a big hall with mattresses covering the floor. No one had a bed to go to; you just had to distinguish which mattress was yours by the color of your clothes or blanket on it.

This young man hosted me without knowing who I was. I thanked him for his kindness and laid my bag on his mattress, then went to take a look outside. Soon it was dinnertime, and everyone got in line. Students were expected to bring their own plates, and I realized that I didn't have one. I ran out to buy one, and when I got back, the food was almost gone. They put one spoonful on my plate, and that was it. I went to find a seat and found one under the trees on some rocks. The more experienced students ate faster and went to get ready for the evening reading that was recommended by the school.

I was still so hungry, but I had to obey the rules. The food was yellow corn *ugali* (similar to mush) and yellow peas, so everything was yellow. For lunch and dinner seven days a week, we were fed the same food. Usually we had no breakfast.

We were watched by the school staff to make sure everyone was in class studying in the evenings. Around nine o'clock was bedtime, and I went to bed wondering what life would look like in that place and was so discouraged by everything I saw there.

Early in the morning, between five and six, everyone had to be out of bed. If you were not, the school staff would come around with sticks in their hands and hit lazy boys who had stayed in bed. Every once in a while, we would get breakfast of plain boiled sorghum flour. During all my morning classes, my only thought was, "When is lunch?" From eight to twelve, it felt like two days.

My second day there, I got my plate and went to sit with some new friends. They introduced me to the others sitting with them and told me about how life was there. They shared some avocados that they had bought on the street with me. They tried to stir up the avocado with our yellow food. What I didn't recognize right away was that there were worms in the food because it was expired.

When I noticed the worms, I quickly asked them if they had seen it. They looked at each other and laughed. "Welcome to ESEKI, Brother Theo," they joked. Right then I knew that was their normal life, and I had to get used to it. We had no choice but to eat it anyway.

DESPERATELY HUNGRY

Life made no sense to me. Every day as I saw all I was going through, while rich people came in vehicles to visit their kids and hand them money to eat in restaurants, I asked myself many questions. I wanted to know who made the rules in life that some people get rich while others are starving to death. What made those rich people different than me? I couldn't see any way of helping myself, so I continued to starve until I got really sick. Even then, there was no one to tell my problems to.

My brother Shyaka, used to take care of me, using his salary to help me pay for school. But because I lied to him, I felt ashamed to come back to him. I wrote a letter, explaining the difficult situation I was going through. He was surprised to know where I went without telling him. I couldn't imagine him reading the letter. The young man who took it to him returned to school, and I hoped he brought good news. But before he handed me the envelope he asked me what I did before I came. As I looked him in the eyes, I knew my brother was offended, so I asked him what my brother had said.

He got so angry and asked the young man, "Where did this letter come from again?" The young man explained the little bit that he knew and told him what I was going through and how badly I needed money. Shyaka looked at him as if he was me. "Go tell him to depend on his own choices or whoever helped him get there." Then he walked away.

The young man said that there was another guy there that looked just like me, and he was so different and peaceful. He said that he had given him the envelope, and he hoped that there was something in there for me. All we hoped for was some money, any amount to buy avocados, because that was the only affordable thing for many of the students.

I opened the envelope with no expectations, but in it was a thousand Rwandan francs (about two U.S. dollars) with some words on a paper. The only thing I remembered written there was, "May Jesus be with you." I knew then that it was my brother Vianney who gave it because he was the first among us to be saved.

Right away, Jesus became my subject to think about. Who was this guy, Jesus? Why do many people talk about him? If He is God, why doesn't He care about me? If He is a man, why do people worship Him?

I went to the forest alone to think about Jesus and tried to test Him with some questions. I was angry about the life I thought I was dealt. I was born a Rwandan in Africa and had suffered since I was born. My parents died, and I had no idea what they had done to deserve such horrendous deaths.

"Where were you, Jesus?" I asked.

Two dollars was a big help to me, and it changed my life. I went to the hospital that evening with a very high fever. One of the nurses saw me sitting down. She looked at my eyes, and her face registered fear. "He is dying," she said. The other nurses came up and took my temperature. I could feel death in me. They treated me fast, and I lived.

I know what it is like to face death. Many people take it lightly and even attempt to take their own lives. Surely they must not know what awaits them after death. Eternity apart from Jesus is an eternity that no man would choose if he really knew the torture of it. Life may seem overwhelming, and some may feel that they just cannot bear the pain of it. But truly the pain of eternity without God is much more than our minds can comprehend and would make our current pain, no matter how severe, seem mild. Jesus is real, and He is the answer for our pain. No problem is too hard for God.

CHAPTER 7
NEW LIFE

A TEST FOR GOD

Through these sufferings, I began to seek a solution because I thought there must be hope for me. Every evening I went to the forest where I could find privacy and thought about myself. I questioned whether God was real or not. I challenged Him to prove Himself to me in many ways, but of course, He didn't jump through my hoops.

Before I gave up, I asked Him to help me with one thing that was too difficult for me to do, even impossible. I knew that if He was able to help me with this, then surely He was real and powerful. That challenge was to pass the national test from level three to level four in secondary school. Level four was a higher, more specialized grade (similar to junior college in America). Up until level three, one have general studies; but starting in level four, one chooses a focus like math or biology.

I thought that was impossible because I had no books and no clue of what was going on in my classes. Because of hunger, I could not sit in class and focus. I was pretending, like many kids did, because you can't study hungry.

Soon the exams were ready for us, and we took buses to the central school where the ministry of education had prepared for our exams. There were police and other security guards to make sure no one cheated. I was so scared because if I failed that test there was no other choice but to repeat the class, studying to retake the test the next year (if I didn't get kicked out). There I was hoping that, if God was real, He might do something for me.

Every time we got out of one of the exams, the students gathered to discuss the tests and how they did. I heard them say things that I put on my papers and was amazed that I might have done well after all. When I was in class, I was only guessing. Sometimes I put something that I heard on the radio, without knowing what it was all about.

God was working in me, but I wasn't sure if He was real. In about a week, we went back home to wait for our results. I did not expect good results for myself.

One day I was sitting in the shop with my brother Shyaka as we waited for customers to come in. A young man came to me full of excitement. "Theo!" he exclaimed. "You passed the test! I found your name on the list."

My brother was surprised and asked him, "Are you sure this guy can pass?"

I didn't believe him either and went to check it out myself. When I went to the district where the results were posted, I spent hours wondering if someone else had the same name as me. I thought he must be the one who passed the test, not me. I went back home hoping it really was me.

GIVING MY LIFE TO JESUS

I still had to wait for the next assignment by the ministry of education. As usual, the government sent students to different schools according to their scores. The school I was assigned to was G. S. Rilima.

When the summer break was over, I went to my new school. I took the bus to Rilima thinking it might be a good place since I heard it was a science school. As soon as I arrived there after a long ride on a muddy road, the bus driver showed me where to go.

I sat down in front of the office, thinking someone would come to welcome me to the school and walk me around to show me the place. I sat there for a long time, and no one came. One of the students asked me if it was my first time at the school. When I told her it was, she smiled really big and told me that no one was going to come to greet me. I had to just go to the boys' dorm and find myself a bed, and then I would be fine. I thanked her, picked up my bag, and went to the boys' dorm.

It was a big hall with a lot of beds without mattresses, and I had no mattress for myself. I sat down on one bed, wondering what was going to happen next. I was hungry and tired, with nowhere to sleep and no one to ask about it.

As I was looking around, I saw a tall, skinny young man at the end of the hallway, who looked familiar to me. So I approached him and tried to introduce myself.

He looked at me with amazement. "Theo, you are here!"

I recognized then that it was a guy I went to school with at Saint Andre. We used to make fun of each other. Now, as he shook my hand, he added, "Praise the Lord Jesus."

I looked at him as if he was a stranger because of the words he spoke. I didn't know what to say but kept watching as he introduced me to his close friend, Richard Buro. I discovered that he went to Saint Andre with me too. They were both known as prideful guys; they only cared about their popularity at the previous school. Now they were acting so differently I thought it was a joke.

They asked if I had found a bed yet. When I told them I hadn't, they made one for me. They gave me their bed covers and everything I needed. Soon it was dark, and we all went together for dinner in the dining room. There was not enough food for the thousand-plus people who lived there, so sometimes students had to fight for it. These two guys helped me and made me feel so welcome. They were very good friends, even though I had nothing to offer them. They made sure I got food and slept well every day.

After dining that first night, we all went out to the basketball court. They began to pray to God, thanking him for bringing me to that school and praying for my protection there. As I watched them, I was amazed again about their transformation. About five more guys joined in. They prayed for two hours with no pause. I got so tired I couldn't wait to go to bed. After their devotional prayers, we went to bed.

They talked about the faithfulness of God with so much joy and happiness. I knew then that these were not the prideful guys I had known anymore, for their lives were changed. I had more peace in that moment than I could remember ever having before. I knew that God must be real, after searching for Him and testing Him for so long.

Early in the morning, about five, they woke me up. I usually hate to wake up that early, but Richard took my blanket off and told me I had to come with them. Getting close to where they took me, I heard a girl with a loud and beautiful voice singing a worship song. They were in a classroom, and they were worshipping God.

I was afraid to enter that room. I let everyone go in before me, and then I went and sat in the back row. Everyone was standing, dancing, and singing with joy. I wasn't used to that, but it felt so good in my heart that it was like having a shower from the inside.

After singing and dancing, they gave an opportunity to whoever had some praises to give. Then one or two people would preach. I thought they were talking about me all the time until I realized that these preachers didn't know anything about me. It was God speaking into my life. I decided to go with them every morning and every evening in the boys' group. As I continued to fellowship with them, I felt so much peace inside that I decided to give my life to Jesus. I was totally free, and joy came into my heart. Since that moment, I have never been the same.

I was so thankful for Magnifique and Richard, the two guys who had taken me under their wings. But I continued to struggle in that school.

WHOM SHALL I SERVE?

I wanted to continue my karate training since I still sought approval from men. I went to visit a students' karate club, and I practiced in the back line, like those who were training for a white belt. I was on the fourth level, but I wanted to surprise the teacher, who was the same level as me.

As I was practicing in the back row, he looked at me and spoke harshly, as if I was making a wrong move. I got angry but waited for one more reason to advance on him. I had a bad wound on my foot that was bothering me, so I wanted to step out of line. In karate, you have to ask permission to step out of line. You do so by bowing your head to the leader to let him know you have a problem, and then he will come to you. I bowed my head to him many times, but he ignored me, so I just stepped out of line and left. He got so angry with me and began to insult me, calling me stupid. I didn't want to cause a big problem, but I ignored his emotion and shamed him in front of his students.

I knew that I was much better than him because I saw his moves and recognized his style. It was a different, less famous style than I had been trained in. The Tiger Club where I had trained was very prestigious and evoked much respect from other clubs.

He told his friends, who were the same level as him, that he didn't like me, and they planned to attack me together. As they were talking about me, a brother of one of the leaders who was against me recognized my name. He told them that I was a teacher in my previous school and how good I was. He exaggerated my skills to them to try to scare them off and to protect me.

It worked and they began to fear me then. They were aware of my skill, and they grew apprehensive to attack me.

I was actually extremely frightened of the thought of their attacks, but when I saw that they began to fear me, I used it to my advantage. I began to talk big, pretending I really was something amazing. I knew that they would send their friends to me to check me out and I would say cocky things like "These guys are risking their lives if they continue like this. I'll kill them."

Even if I knew that my training had been more advanced than theirs, I knew that if even just two of them attacked me together I would be put to shame. I continued to keep up my act because I was so afraid that they might really attack me. I was like many big mouth people that I have since encountered in my life. Often those who are consumed with fear try to invoke fear in those around them to cover their own. We reproduce fear that is first sewn in us.

Soon I started my own club at Rilima, and the whole school came to watch me teach. The other club decided to join mine too. The leaders of the other club were not willing to join at that time, but some of them came to talk to me. We discussed the issue that I had with their friend. I found them so humble; I decided to work with them. Soon they noticed that my techniques were so smart and higher than theirs, and they voted for me to teach.

Knowing that the whole school respected me, I was torn about who I should hang out with. Should I choose those preachers who helped me get close to God and find peace, or the fighters who made me feel like the most honored student in the whole school?

I began to wonder if karate was a sin or if I could practice and go to church at the same time. I continued to struggle with my choices.

It wasn't karate that I loved so much but the pride that I got from it. My only focus was to make people more impressed with me and to get more attention from girls. I loved it when I heard that people were talking about how I could beat up ten guys at once and how no one could challenge me. This was not actually the truth about me, but the inflated reputation that I had helped to create.

I had my own exhibition to show people how great I was and went to other schools to perform my karate moves. I began to miss Sunday worship and began to lose connection with God. Instead, I connected with unbelievers, who only encouraged me to drink and get some pretty girls. I was disconnected from the people who showed me what life was for real and showed me the love of God.

This was a battle for me because I wasn't feeling God in my life and had no peace about what I was doing. It felt like I was worshiping another god, which was true. I was more interested in my own glory than I was in glorifying God. You can't serve two kings, for you will please one and cause the other to anger.

This school was like a garage where God sent me to be fixed. I learned how to run from seeking my own glory and to reserve that for God. I learned to humble myself and become a servant of God and his people.

Richard was a very smart preacher, and he made me feel like I was good without karate, but he never told me to change. Instead he helped me to change with his wisdom. He often gave me good counsel during this time in my life. The more I sought my own glory, the worse I made my situation.

One time, we went out to celebrate the anniversary of a school that had invited us to perform our techniques, and we spent a night there. I was the leader and the best performer, so everyone waited for me to perform the following morning. That night I struggled in my spirit when everyone was going out to have fun, and I stayed in bed alone. The other guys went out with beautiful girls from that school, and they asked me many times if I could come with them. There were girls waiting for me, but I couldn't find the peace to get out the door. Finally they left me in the room, struggling with my heart. I knew then that I wasn't where I was supposed to be.

There in that small world I looked like a superstar. When someone is exalted, it becomes easy for them to fall into a pit of pride. God resists the proud, but to the humble he gives freely.

When I came back to school, I sat down and thought of the choice I was about to make that was going to change my life completely. If I quit karate, I would lose my career and my respect among people. I was getting close to being a champion someday. If I quit following Jesus, I knew then that hell would be waiting for me, and my peace would be gone forever.

I felt hope to succeed with either of those choices, but I remembered what my friend George often preached in our student meetings. He quoted 1 Timothy 4:8: "For physical training is of some value, but godliness has value for all things, holding promise for both the present life and the life to come."

George always gave examples of me in church. He talked about how he liked my passion when I trained myself in karate and how I used all my energy to reach my goals. He was so smart. He would always make me feel encouraged, but he never hid the truth from me. He would tell others to exercise their spirits the way I exercised my body in karate. He encouraged every Christian to train themselves in spiritual matters with all their efforts. This challenged me because the Spirit inside of me was already telling me that I was losing in spiritual matters to gain in physical and worldly matters.

I prayed and fasted for many days to give my whole being to God so that I would be able to reach my spiritual goals even if lost my reputation. I began to miss many karate practices and performances because of church programs until my fellow students in karate began to challenge me. They wanted to know if I was one of them or one of those crazy Jesus freaks.

One night I had a dream that my leg was getting cut off. I screamed and asked God to please heal me, and I would never go back to karate. When I opened my eyes, I was so sad because I didn't want to give up karate. Something inside of me still wanted to have my own power. Even though I was saved, pride kept knocking at the door of my heart. It was up to me to decide if I opened it or not.

The next day I went back to the karate club. The strongest, most skilled student came up to me and wanted to spar with me. We began, and soon a crowd formed. Looking at his face, I could tell he wanted to kick my leg, and I remembered my dream the night before.

I told him, "Stop, I forgot something. Wait." I took my belongings and left for good, never going back to karate. Karate was an idol to me, and I had to give it up because I don't want to have something that stands between my God and me.

At first I told the students in karate club that I was one of them, but I also loved Jesus and wanted to give Him my whole life. I even tried to preach to them, but I was still double-minded.

DRAMATIC CHANGE

When the leaders of the student ministry found me faithful in what I was doing and saw a big change in my life, they asked me to share my testimony with the student church. That whole week before I was supposed to speak, I was praying and fasting and scared of speaking in front of people. I had never spoken in front of a group of believers before and was so scared.

It was life-changing for me when I did speak because God put the words in my mouth. After the service, they told me that the words I spoke were in the Bible. I didn't know the Bible very well at that time, but God was speaking to my heart. What a God we serve! How could God use such a stubborn and rebellious sinner like me? I can't even begin to explain the joy that experience brought into my life, knowing that God can use me the same way he used the Apostle Paul and so many others in the Bible. After my fellow karate students heard that I preached in church, they gave up on me and let me go.

Life meant nothing to me without Christ. I decided to follow Jesus and do whatever it took for me to be a blameless Christian. The teachings of the men and women in the student-led church were so challenging, and they helped me become a big influence in the community. I traveled around the town preaching the Good News of the God, who gave me joy.

When I decided to completely follow Jesus, I began to notice others who seemed to have one foot in the kingdom of God and one foot in the world, just as I had before. I didn't know that there were strong and weak Christians. I thought that all Christians were strong and I was alone in my previous struggle. They all seemed so strong in our fellowships, and then I began to notice their weakness outside the fellowships. Because I had just made the decision to change my life and no longer be double-minded, I really began to notice those who were double-minded.

Soon I began to work with many of them who had what we called "bad fruits." I asked my leaders if that was possible, and they told me that it happens very often. My first Christian friend and pastor, Richard, was passionate about fully living for Christ and changing the lives of people like me. Christian choirs are large ministries in Rwanda. He encouraged me to be in a choir with him because we wanted to correct the errors that we found in it, and it wasn't easy to make a change while we were outside the choir.

Neither one of us were very good singers, so we prayed to God for favor as we waited for our applications to be accepted by the choir leaders. Soon, we were accepted and began to practice with them for a probationary period before we were pronounced members of the choir. Our goal wasn't to be singers, but to have a chance to make a change. God enabled us to sing well, and we enjoyed it very much.

Very soon they voted for new leaders of the choir, and they voted for me as counselor. It didn't take long until I became the counselor of the whole congregation. That is when I approached many people who showed bad fruits.

We knew that some of them were sexually involved and engaging in lustful activities, even though they were choir leaders, so I decided to take action. I approached each of them individually first about their activities, but they refused to listen to me. I then invited the leaders of the choir and the church to come together for a meeting. At that meeting I called out the president, who was acting shamefully and exposed her actions. She confessed in front of the group and left the choir.

The choir originally had about thirty people, but when I started to stop those whose hearts were so worldly, all that remained were eight members. I approached all the rest, who were shaming our group, and asked them to step down until they got their lives right.

I can't remember any other time we had revival, like we did when those eight people sang in the congregation. I became the leader of this choir that became like a church in our school. People outside the school asked permission to come and fellowship with us. We became a bigger church, and God manifested Himself among us, even though we were not very educated in theology. God was enough for us and gave everyone who preached the words to speak. I spent all my time seeking God to fill me while He tested and examined me.

There were times when I wondered if I had made the right decision because I missed the attention that I got from worldly things before I fully committed to Christ. I kept my faith that God would repay me with the greatest reward for my obedience to Him. My old friends never quit trying to convince me that I was foolish to trust in something that I could not see, but I felt something inside telling me to never give up. I could see hope even though I couldn't explain it. I guess that is what we call faith.

Life in Rilima needed something to hope for. The school itself was not offering much hope. Most of the time, we had no teachers, and we almost always were short on food. I had nowhere else to go, like many of the other students there, so we stayed there wondering what our futures would entail.

I was questioned a lot because I had given up what appeared to be of great value for something that many people considered of no value. I knew that I was not a fool, because I had given up something that had no eternal value for the greatest treasure of all—life in Christ.

On the other side, my family was so happy with who I had become and how my life was so honest and reliable. They were still concerned about my future and my schooling. School was not going so well for me because of all the struggles we had. They thought I prayed too much and forgot to study, but even the leaders testified about how I spent a lot of time studying.

Makombe family: Clockwise from top: Theo, Shema, Sifa, Bell, Bri (the youngest, Remy is not pictured).

Makombe family: Left to right: Sifa, Theo, Shema, Bri, Bell (the youngest, Remy is not pictured).

Memorial Wall for lives lost in the Genocide.
This wall is dedicated to Theo's aunt and her children that were lost.
It reads: Mwizerwa Mukankwaya Eugenie, Her Children:
The names of her children lost in the genocide are then listed with
the year of their birth. Theo's cousin, Shyaka Theoneste, is the only
surviving member of this family. Because this family was one of
the wealthier families in town, their deaths were very torturous.

VICTIMS OF GENOCIDE,
"Brothers and Sisters you've been characterized by"

Love~Dignity~Faithfulness

The names listed below are family members of
those listed in the other picture that tried to hide
together with the family of Shyaka Theoneste.

Banana Trees very much like the ones that Theo hid among.

The only surviving picture of Theo from the time around
the genocide. This pictures was taken less than a year after
the killings. He is pictured here with his aunt Janete.

CHAPTER 8
YOU CAN'T STAND ON BOTH SIDES

TWO OPPOSING POWERS

Growing up, I knew two different powers, opposite powers. Now I know that every human being in the world is in a battle, and each is called to choose a side. In my hometown, there were people we were warned about as kids—to never go to their houses, greet them, or take anything that they gave to us—because they were dangerous people. However, these people were active, like anyone else. They went to the same market as we did, participated in the same activities, and even went to the same churches. The only reason I was told they were dangerous was because they practiced witchcraft. That was scary to me, but I knew nothing about witches. I thought that was just another kind of life.

Witchcraft was a normal part of our lives. Many practiced it, and unusual events were often attributed to it. Sometimes on my way home, I would see piles of food and money on the side of the road. I was always told to never touch them because they were traps, and if I touched them, I could die. They were mostly candies so that kids would be interested. Surely some kids died, or even adults died from other kinds of traps.

It was common in Rwanda for pregnant women to be cursed by witchdoctors so that their pregnancy would continue longer than it should have—sometimes very, very long. The last pregnancy that my mom had, she was struck by a witchdoctor, even though we never knew who had cursed her. She was pregnant for over a year with my little brother and was hospitalized for a very long time, yet no one knew that she was pregnant.

Finally, the traditional doctors came to help her. They brought their stuff and sucked the metal out of her body, and she was released from those powers. Soon she had a baby boy. We were so surprised when she came home with a baby because none of us knew that she was pregnant. They called him Emmanuel (God with us) as my father commanded.

Now my father believed in God and warned us to never practice witchcraft or go to a witch for any counsel. However, I still don't think these doctors who came to help were natural or from God; I think they operated spiritually. No doctor was able to help my mother, and the things they did to her were very strange.

Many witches competed against each other. If you were cursed by one, you had to go to another to help you.

I have heard many people talking about government leaders that consult witchdoctors regularly. One I heard about often was Mobutu, the former president of Congo. I don't think that there is any way that Habyalimana Juvenal could have carried out preparations for such a horrific mass murder over a span of thirty years if he had not been influenced by true evil. We can listen to people talking about the evil in government leaders, but all we have to do is look at their fruit to judge for ourselves. The king of this world is surely at work. We can sugarcoat it and call it civil war or political conflicts, but evil will always be evil.

I call it the kingdom of darkness. The king of that kingdom appears in different forms, depending on the region, country or culture. He knows what pleases men, and he uses everything their flesh desires to trap their minds. The love of money is truly the root of all kinds of evil (2 Timothy 6:10). I have seen money make many people deny their own relatives and friends—even causing the death of those they loved—to gain riches.

In 2008, we went to the northern province of Uganda, near Sudan. We stayed there for two weeks in an Internally Displaced

Peoples Camp. The people in the camp were the victims of another power-hungry man highly influenced by evil, who was leading mass killings.

From day one, I was told that there was a group of rebel soldiers led by a guy named Joseph Kony, who was filled with evil spirits and called his group the Lord's Resistance Army, or LRA. Even though the group was formed to "free" the Acholi people of Northern Uganda and southern Sudan, it was mainly the Acholi people that they attacked. They brutalized them in horrific ways, from murder and mutilation to cannibalism. The army claimed that they were led by the Lord to commit such atrocities, but it is evident that the kingdom of darkness was at work among them.

If the politics of a nation are evil, then the whole land is under curses. Can you imagine being under the leadership of that kind of person who has no love or compassion for people, but does what the devil tells him to do? I know what he would do. He would kill as many people as he can because the enemy Satan comes to steal, kill and destroy. We have so many people without a conscience trying to make their mark in history. We have to be very careful with every decision we make when we vote.

THE BLAME GAME

In my life I had been involved in the things of God and the things of the devil. After I gave my life fully to the Lord, I understood how clearly they were divided. Some people say that they are not involved; they don't care. They say they just want to be a good person and mind their own business.

Have you ever seen a soldier stand between two sides on the battlefield and not get hurt? This world is a battlefield. Which side are you on? You have to be brave and fight or be fearful and lazy, but know that you may be taken over and defeated.

When the devil takes captives, he trains them to blame God for their afflictions. He tells them that God failed to save them, failed to prosper them, failed to save the loved ones they lost. He is raising his army to fight against the kingdom of light because of the greed for power that was his downfall.

That is where I was stuck for a long time. Instead of worshiping God and thanking Him for sparing my life from the evil one, I blamed Him for letting my loved ones be murdered as though God did it Himself.

If I think about the people in my life that have habitually blamed God, I can see what their lives have become. Some are dead. Some are in prison. Many are in extreme poverty. They think God made them suffer, while He made others live well in peace and prosperity.

It is so dangerous to grumble against God. Satan is always ready to fill our heads with lies disguised as truth to make us enemies of God. This is why I work hard to tell the children of God that God loves them, and it's not too late for them to come back to life. After I lived in the dark and found light, I began a spiritual fight that resulted in the huge deliverance of many.

CONFRONTING THE ENEMY

One time when I was first trying to exercise the supernatural power of God, there was a young man who was possessed by an evil spirit that caused him to fight and run all day long. He was one of the students at Rilima, and he was so strong that no one was able to help him or even catch him. I asked God to help him through me, and I approached him once and talked to him. It was a surprise for many to see me talking to him, even though it wasn't him talking, but the demon inside of him. I asked the demon to release the young man, but the demon refused, and I began to fast for this boy.

Later I learned that he had been given to a demon by his mother, who practiced witchcraft. I continued to pray, until I was the only person that demon feared in the whole town. Every time I approached the boy and told him to calm down, he did. I washed and clothed him with my clothes.

Because I was busy at school, I rented a house outside of the school. I left him sleeping there and came to bring him food after school or at break time. After the demon found out the boy was getting well and normal, he decided to steal him away while I was in class. I never had a chance to see the young man again. I was so sad that I lost the battle because I had to be in school. I never wanted to let anything make me too busy for the kingdom of God, but school was there.

Several times I went close to the lake behind the school, where the spirits of witchcraft manifested in the evening. Often I saw a fire across the lake and wondered what it was, but I decided to command the fire to stop, to see whether it was natural or supernatural. Every time I said, "Stop," the fire across the lake disappeared. Then I knew we were under attack from spiritual powers.

For the first time I was beginning to realize the spiritual battle that was all around us. I also began to understand the authority that we have because of Jesus. I began to see more and more evidence of spiritual warfare all around me.

Many students were having problems in their dorms, having terrible dreams, and being attacked by demons more often, so I decided to be the watchman through intercessory prayer. Many were rescued by God's power, but they refused to acknowledge that it was God who helped them and credited their healing to coincidence.

One night, I remember well, I was sleeping in my bedroom at that school, where about one thousand students stayed—girls on one side and boys on the other. The spirit of God woke me up, and I went to pray in the classroom around one in the morning. While I was still praying, one of the teachers came close because I was praying aloud. I thought I was in trouble, but that was not the case. I don't know how he felt, but he stayed behind the door waiting for me. I was taking a long time, so he found a young boy who was going to read in the night. He sent him to ask me if I could come outside because he needed help.

I came out with confidence and asked, "Teacher, how may I help you?"

He was shaking and began to tell me the situation. His fellow teacher's wife was found dead in her living room around 6:00 p.m. It was getting late, while they prayed over her, but nothing happened. Some of them were drunk; others were just afraid because they didn't know how she died or how to explain it to the police.

They decided to find someone who prays to God to help them. I didn't know how she died or how to help them. But I was found faithful to them, so I honored their faith. I thought I needed to know her story. When I asked the teacher about her, he told me that every year, her family expected to lose someone because they believed some demons were sent to kill one member of the family every year as a sacrifice. I knew that the woman was a victim and wasn't involved in any evil, which gave me the right to pray for her.

I woke up two prayer warriors, Brother Enoch and Brother John. They were my prayer partners, who never questioned me about anything I said, even if I got them up in the middle of the night. They came with me to the house of the teacher.

We entered and asked the teachers to go outside. We prayed for the woman to live, even though she was dead, and she came back to life. The next thing the teachers heard was a woman's voice talking to us, and they were all filled with fear as we came out. Nobody would say a word because they were afraid of us.

We were filled with joy after we left the house, but we told no one about it because no one would have believed us. The teachers believed the miracle, and the woman still lives today.

I praise God for the victories he gave us as we fought to reclaim Rilima for him. I grew so much in this time as I prayed, worshiped and fought with some amazing men of God. I look back on this time and am so thankful for the spiritual education that God gave me there.

After Rilima, I went to another school where there was clear spiritual warfare. I started an intercession group there because their other student ministries were falling apart. The director was a pastor and wanted the students to know God, but so many were so deceptive. They would come and sing in the choir or lead fellowship, but it was almost all for show.

Shortly after I started the intercession group, we planned a whole night of prayer. While we were praying in the middle of the night, one of the girls in the choir got attacked by demons in her room. She was thrown to the ground and became paralyzed. Other students carried her to us where we were praying. She was not the first one in that school to be attacked in that way, so they were aware of what was happening.

One of the other students who had been praying with us was experienced in deliverance and began to question the demons inside of her. He asked them where they came from, and they told him that they were sent to her by her mother. They tried to convince us that they could not be cast out because they had a powerful base in her mother's home and were sent on a mission. The demons refused to leave and said that they were going to kill her.

We commanded them to come out of her in the name of Jesus. They did not come out right away, and the student experienced in deliverance continued to question them. After about half an hour of commanding them, the spirits left, and the girl was restored. The entire time that we were fighting the demons, she had remained in a paralyzed state.

CHOOSING SIDES

If you want to live a good life, it will be one you fight for, not one you get by chance. Many people experience what they call "good luck." I assure you there is only God's power to protect them, as we pray for the nations every day, and the God of mercy hears and protects us according to his word.

Jesus said, "In this world you will have trouble. But take heart! I have overcome the world" (John 16:33). This means that we have help from Jesus if we believe in Him and we know that living in the world is to live in a battlefield. Ignoring the battle will not make it go away, but it will surely give ground to the enemy in your life. Tribulations come to all.

Satan likes those who don't care. They lose, and they will accuse God. My younger brother, Felicien, when he was very young, used to play hide and seek. He didn't really understand the game and would just hide his eyes. He thought that if he couldn't see you, you couldn't see him. This is how it is for people of this world who say they don't believe in demons or in the Holy Spirit. Saying that you don't believe in them doesn't change the fact that they exist. These people don't see anything, so they think nobody sees them.

Jesus said, "He who is not with me is against me, and he who does not gather with me scatters" (Matthew 12:30). This is why people all over the world worship demons without knowing what they are doing—mostly through entertainment and other cultural celebrations.

When I was a teenager, I wanted to be powerful all on my own, so I began to learn karate. I was afraid, because of my past, and I wanted to defend myself, if I was ever attacked again. I began to go into the forest alone to meditate. I created war in my mind until the other students thought that I was the devil. I began to fight people, just to try out my skills. I wanted to be a superman.

My teacher was already incredible. I was told that he could levitate by meditation of evil spirits. He disappeared for some time, after we were told that he sacrificed his mother to this evil spirit and killed his friend who knew his secret. Everybody knew it. I was ready to travel down the same road as him because I thought I needed extra power to protect myself.

Satan is a terrorist but is also very cunning. If you are not strong enough to stand up for truth and righteousness, you will become his slave, whether you know it or not. You were made to be with your Creator twenty-four hours a day to be His pleasure. There is no better pleasure than to be in the presence of God. You cannot truly fear God and still fear man. If you fear God, you should be afraid of nothing else.

In 1 John 4:4, the Lord reminds us, "You, dear children, are from God and have overcome them, because the one who is in you is greater than the one who is in the world." It is clear in that verse that there are two sides. There is a positive side—in which everyone is created to belong—and a negative one in which we are deceived. There are two kingdoms reigning now, but it's your choice to be on the weak side or the strong side.

CHAPTER 9
LEARNING TO WALK IN
INTEGRITY AND FAITH

FEELING LESS THAN HUMAN

After the war, I was treated very poorly because I had no one to defend me. As an orphan, there were scholarships available to me so that I could go to secondary school. In order to get a scholarship, I had to go to the government office and apply for it. Sometimes I would travel for several hours to get to the office. Many times I had to walk because I didn't have money for bus fare. When I got there, the officials often ignored me and would pretend I was not there. I had no adult to represent me, and they paid no attention to me, because of my young age and low social status. Many rich kids or students from influential families got scholarships with no problem. But poor kids like me, who needed them the most, were pushed aside and trampled on.

There were so many times I would tell those in charge something, but they pretended they never heard me. Often I waited for someone who was talking in the hallway with coworkers, sitting at their desk taking a social phone call, or laughing with others until they came out to take a break. It didn't matter if the document I needed would save my life. They would have let me die because I was nobody to them. I saw many people go in with nice suits and get everything they needed very quickly, but for me, it was a waste of time.

Sometimes I wondered if these people had ever been in my situation. I hoped God would choose people who had suffered so they would know how to help others who were going through the same things. Now I know that He does choose such people.

When I went to school the first time after the genocide, the other kids made fun of me. I began to feel like an animal, not a human, because I couldn't have confidence in myself anymore. When I lost my mind and memories, forgetting what time of day it was, not knowing who I was anymore, that is when I doubted my humanity. I would pinch my skin to see if I could feel pain, but still I couldn't believe who I had become.

Going to school late was okay. Anyone can be late, even every day, but going to school during Christmas break or other holidays was so insane. That is what I did many times. I told no one what was going on in my life for many years, but God still had good plans for my future—even when, to me, the future was not an option.

I never thought of myself as somebody who could someday give hope to the nations because I needed hope for myself. God always sees a way, where there seems to be none. That is what gives me hope, knowing that when my weaknesses increase, God's strength will increase even more. Then I don't have to be afraid of anything.

DEALING WITH CORRUPTION

In the school I attended, many of the teachers were very corrupt. They would purposely make the tests nearly impossible to pass because students would pay them for points, so that they could pass. Before I was saved, I paid them and passed many tests when others didn't. One teacher would come to me before a test and tell me that it was going to be very hard and that none of us could pass. I would pay him before the test, and I would pass, while all of the other students who did not pay failed.

When I was in school failing, one of my fellow Christians came to me and gave me ideas on how I should try the other way that was corrupt to help me get to college easily. They created false documents and sold them to people, as if they passed the test. This was not just black market, but even church people did this.

There are so many Christians who struggle with wrong attitudes, such as, "Let me try just once" or "Everybody does it." But these are all lies of the enemy.

For me, that was harder than to keep on trying in my weakness. My integrity was worth more than a false paper.

I lost support of school fees from the government fund for orphans and survivors of the genocide my last year in secondary school. *Hey, you know what?* I told myself. *This is not my business. If God has made me, He knows what is wrong with me. He knows what is for me and what is not.*

The school threw me out, but I could feel something powerful in me, and I couldn't give it up. People tried to help me move forward to live my life with a little bit of lies. I refused, saying that I would not live a lie. I needed the truth. Some of them gave me false papers to cheat my way to a better life.

"No," I said. "You want me to try a lie. Why not try the truth?"

A TOUGH TURN OF EVENTS

In 2005, I decided to keep on trying school because I still had some fears in life. There was no other door open for me. I went to ask my school director if he could give me a last chance to finish high school and get a diploma, even though that was so hard for me since I was forced to study in a section that did not interest me. I knew for sure that God never called me to do anything similar to what I was studying, but I forced myself again because there was no other door open. The director gave me my chance after the head of studies in that school sent me home for good.

I packed all my belongings and went to take a bus to the boarding school. At the bus stop, I got robbed, and the thief took everything I had, including the notebooks for the past four years of school, which I needed to prepare for the national exams. This was a big test to me, missing a diploma that I worked for many years, but failing in the end.

This happened five years after I decided to try and follow Jesus. I walked around, trying to find a clue of how I could recover my suitcase, but it was impossible. Everything I owned was gone. I had nothing left but the clothes I was wearing.

As I walked in and out of the bus station, a motorbike taxi came up and almost hit me. The rider looked at me as if I was crazy, but he didn't say anything. I looked at the front of the motorbike, and there was a verse written: "Cast your burden upon Jesus, for he cares for you."

Now I was angry with God and didn't want to hear anything from Him, but I didn't want to backslide. I went inside the bus station, thinking that maybe if I went upstairs and stood on the front porch where I could see the whole station, there might be a chance I could spot anybody who was carrying my suitcase out. Plus, I wanted to be alone, without people or God.

As I stood there, I was surprised by loud music behind me. There was a big speaker for commercials because they play songs louder to get customers. A Christian song was playing. The words of the song went something like this:

This is why I never give up waiting on the Savior.
Therefore I do not lose heart.
Though outwardly I am wasting away,
Yet inwardly I am being renewed day by day.

I didn't want to hear biblical words again. I thought God had forsaken me, but hope came back to me, even without my belongings, still homeless and still dealing with many other struggles of life. I called my brother, who got saved before me, and I told him what happened.

"Is there anything I can do to help?" he asked.

"No. I just wanted to tell you that."

Right away I went to a church near the bus station to try God again since He always sees us and may have had the best for me. There in the church an old friend saw me coming in and out.

He followed me and said, "Hi, Theo, good to see you again."

"Why?" I couldn't understand why it would be good to see me.

He replied, "You are the strongest man of faith that I know, and I need to hear from you. I am struggling a lot." He was struggling with life, losing hope, despised by the people around him. He had been working for food as a house boy.

While he shared his problems with me, the power of the Holy Spirit rushed on me, and I began to talk to him. "My friend, this is how God teaches us. We will be a great people, and many shall depend on us." I continued with the Scripture from the song: even though our outer selves are wasting away, our inner selves are being renewed. I also told him why I was not at school and what had happened.

He stopped walking and started to breath harder "Oh, Theo, I am sorry. I didn't know what was happening in your life, and here you are trying to comfort me."

"No, it's okay. You just told me how strong I am in faith. So be it." As I encouraged him, I felt so much stronger, and we both grew in hope together.

The Bible says, "Give thanks to the LORD, for he is good; his love endures forever" (Psalms 106:1). We don't give thanks to God because He did what we told Him to do; we thank Him because He deserves it. Even when He is testing us, we need to praise Him. For His grace is always enough for us, and He makes all things work together for our good.

We took a long walk to his boss's house. He cooked some food for us, and after we ate, we spent some time praying. After that, I left and tried to find another way to go back to school in Rilima. That place was truly bound with my heart since I had seen how people received Christ and many miracles. Signs and wonders followed the Gospel that I preached there, and that made me feel so alive that I didn't care much about my failure.

I had enough money for a one-way ticket to Rilima, so I took off the next morning. When my brothers and sisters in Christ saw me, they rejoiced greatly. We had many more good fellowships and preached to many more people there. Glory be to God, who gives us strength, when we are crushed in spirit!

NEW DIRECTION

Many of my teachers told me that I spent too much time with God, so I failed in science. That was not true. They were just accusing me with lies.

I spent days and nights trying to work for a diploma, even though I had lost everything and had no books or money to buy more. I did all that was possible, with all of my strength. I even remember one of the leaders calling me to come into his office, where he asked what was wrong with me. He told me that he had been watching me day and night reading books, but I still failed. "Theo, what is going wrong?"

My answer was simple. I just repeated what he had said about me studying day and night and replied, "You must know more than me. I don't know why I am failing. I am trying as hard as I can."

He advised me to change sections and choose an easy one. Honestly, I was still waiting for God's direction and didn't know what was best for me. I knew that I was supposed to preach the Good News the rest of my life, but I didn't know how to handle life in general. Financially, I was falling apart, and life was getting harder.

Before I got saved, I spent time in night clubs and in bars drinking, but nobody confronted me for doing anything wrong. But when I spent more time praying and seeking my God and the truth about life, everyone was concerned about me and thought I was crazy.

"Better is one day in the house of the Lord than a thousand elsewhere" (Psalms 84:10). It seems odd to many when a person spends so much of their time seeking the Lord. But those that find Him understand that, truly, a day with the Lord is better than thousands without Him.

I studied and preached the Good News to many people. Many gave their lives to God very seriously because I made sure that the people were really becoming Christians. About two months before I was to take the national test, I had a dream. I was late for a school that looked like a national university. When I got there, the leaders came to welcome me and asked me how I was doing and why I came late. Even though I was told in my dream that I was at a university, it looked different than any university that I knew.

After my dream, God sent a prophet that I trusted very much. He told me what was real and going on in my life and asked me to come with him to the place where God told him to take me. The prophet God sent was a very simple man and a former student of the same high school. He is the one who led me to Christ, Richard Buro.

After he told me that, I said good-bye to those I led and to my friends in Christ. By the Spirit of God, I told them that God said He was taking me to the university. They asked me about it and what the name was, but I didn't know. So they asked me how sure I was and what kind of university was. Then by the Spirit, I told everybody there that the university I was going to was only for those who believe in Jesus.

I left my friends in tears and went with my best friend Richard. He took me to Discipleship Training School (DTS) with Youth with a Mission (YWAM). When we got there, I recognized the grounds of the school and was trying to remember when I had been there before. Then I remembered that I had seen it in my dream.

That is where God transformed my mess into a message, and I was certified by the University of the Nations. Maybe the world sees things differently and has everything set in a worldly way, but God always has His ways to teach His people.

My victory is not that I got everything that I wanted, not even that I became a great minister; my victory is that I am still standing, doing God's will. And all who have been against me turned back to me.

BEYOND MY ABILITY

Many churches in Africa are also very corrupt. It is common for pastors to start a church as a business, not a ministry, and to only seek their own prosperity. For that reason, most churches in Rwanda do not support missions. They want to keep money and people in their churches. When I felt called to do a DTS, I went to my pastor, but he did not support me. He said that if I wanted to learn more about serving God, I just had to come and sit down in Sunday morning services, and he would teach me.

I promised God to live a truthful life so that I could show the world that none who trusted in Him would ever be put to shame. Now I was being tested, as if I was put to shame myself. What people call shame is not true. Instead they call good evil and evil good because the world knows nothing about the truth.

We studied for three months in the classroom in YWAM and the last two months of our schooling were on the mission field. We all had to pay school fees and everyone was paying some amount of money, but for me, it seemed like every door was closed. Whoever I thought of as my supporter would reject me and accuse me of craziness. Proverbs 19:22 says, "[It is] better to be poor than a liar."

One time I was cleaning a classroom and thinking about how I could find support. I was the only student in my school who had not paid any school fees at all. In order to go on the outreach phase of our schooling, I had to pay some amount of school fees. I felt so tired and lay on the floor because I was so discouraged with my life. There was a German girl, a fellow student, who came to me and handed me ten thousand Rwandan francs, which was about twenty US dollars. She said that she felt God leading her to give me that to support me in my school fees.

I went quickly to my leader and asked her, "Would you please let me go to outreach? Here is ten thousand!"

She looked at me with so much happiness. "Where did you get this money, Theo?"

I was happy to explain how I was lying on the floor, questioning God, when this young lady came to me and handed me the money that He had told her to give. My leader and I both rejoiced, for she had been praying for me and very much wanted me on her team.

Soon outreach began. Before we took off from the base, she came and informed me that God had told her that I was the watchman, or spiritual leader, of the team. It made me so happy that even though many people saw me as crazy, these missionaries saw me as a spiritual man.

The next test was when we returned from outreach and graduated. I wanted to leave the base as soon as possible and try to find a job so that I could pay my school fees. I knew that God called me to work with Youth with a Mission, but I was worried about my finances. I had not yet been able to pay my school fees, and I could not imagine how I would be able to pay staff fees as well.

This was one of the times I had to try another level of faith. God didn't provide everything that I needed at one time because He was taking me higher. Usually we can only have faith as far as we can imagine, and it is difficult to believe for something beyond our imaginations. When God is taking us to the next level of faith, He often takes us in our current situations and shows us what to have faith for. Otherwise we can stay on the same level, believing in what we can accomplish ourselves.

It is most often scary for us to be in new situations where we cannot figure anything out. God alone is the only One that can help us. These are the moments we learn how to be friends with Him, when we have no other friend but Him alone.

My friends used to come to me, asking me how I felt about my trials because they couldn't believe it. They told me that I ignored everything as if it were not there. That was a little encouragement, but then inside of me, I was troubled to see people succeed in many things that I was able to do myself, but had to wait on God. This is personal faith. It can work for you, but you can't share it with anyone else.

When the wisdom of men surrounds you, you find yourself logically so stupid but still following God's voice, wondering if He will ever repeat what He said to make sure He is with you. That is not how it works for God's followers. He expects you to believe even when you can't see.

One day after I had graduated from the mission school, I was walking out of the gates, and I heard a voice calling my name. I got scared because I was escaping because I had no staff fees but I didn't have anywhere to go to. I could not bear to live off of other people anymore.

I turned around, and it was Uncle Richard, who was the base leader at the time. He was also a prophet, whom I never once heard prophesying with doubt or fear. Whatever he said happened quickly.

I went back to him, and he asked me where I was going. We both knew in our spirit that I was running away from the mission. I told him my plans, and he assured me that I wasn't going to succeed out there.

He asked me to stay so he could speak with me the next day. I stayed until the next morning. I was waiting for him to come by, but it was getting late. Soon I discovered that he had flown to the United Kingdom that same day. I was even more discouraged, so I decided to go back on my plans.

As I was walking out of the dining room, I met the national leader, Method. I never expected him to know my situation. He greeted me and asked me to sit down with him for a talk. I knew nothing about him. I had just seen him around a few times. He was usually traveling around the world.

"Well, Theo, Richard asked me to talk to you, and I don't know what to talk about," he started. He asked me if I had ever heard God calling me to work with YWAM. I said that maybe He had, but I was not able. He asked me why, and I told him my concerns about school and staff fees.

Looking beyond my knowledge, he gave me his testimony of how he had come to YWAM. I was touched to know that he was simple, like anyone else, and he was willing to help me.

He asked me to fill out the form for a staff position if I made the decision to work with them and believe in God like he did. I agreed, but as soon as we separated, before I filled out the forms, I ran away. I had a little money in my pocket and had a project for it. I wanted to work on my own support as if God was not able anymore.

Soon my money was gone by taking the buses, like Richard had prophesied to me. He told me not to waste my time trying to get money in the secular world because I would not be successful. He said that God had a plan for me in His ministry. I had no other choice but to obey God and go where He wanted me to be—at Youth with a Mission.

I returned to YWAM and took a position on staff of the next Discipleship Training School. I still felt so weak and unable, but it gave me so much joy to know that the leaders believed in me and I trusted God to carry me.

We trained many students, and we took them on outreaches in different nations. That was the hardest work I had ever done in my mission experience, but I also saw God's hand in my life and in students, whose lives were transformed through this discipleship program.

CHAPTER 10
INTERCULTURAL LOVE STORY

A BOLD AND DESPERATE PRAYER

In 2006, I was tired and weary and needed new strength. I prayed for God to open doors for my ministries. I had visions that I knew came from God, but it seems like, when you think something is going to work for you, you frequently lose it and have to start over again. I was expecting God to open the door and help me do what He told me to.

I was not being the father I needed to be to the child I had conceived with my cousin, yet I had no time for her. My failures were increasing every day. She came to stay with me for several weeks around Christmas, and we both loved that time. Some of my family came to me at the YWAM base and told me I couldn't take care for a child yet. They said I needed to grow up, and after some years, maybe I could have her when she was older. I didn't know how I could do anything in ministry before I had taken care of the ministry that God had already given me—my daughter.

On December 31, 2006, I was getting ready to go to a New Year's Eve celebration in a local church. I sat down in my room around 8:00 p.m. and prayed, "God, I have your vision, but I don't even have anyone to talk to about how I feel. Who is going to be part of this?" This was a very big issue to me because I was focusing on God's work but forgetting my own needs.

As I asked God who was going to be on my side, I heard His voice telling me, "Get married, and share it with your wife."

That sounded impossible, but I thought if it was God, then I had to believe. My first worry was how in the world I was going to convince one of these girls outside of the mission to come and suffer with me. I never thought of another missionary girl because I already had some others in mind who loved me too. However, I never heard God telling me who it was going to be.

So I prayed, "If it's really you, God, give me a fiancée in this next month, and next year I will marry her."

I thanked God for His idea and left the room. As I walked out, the Spirit led me to the dining room, where foreign missionaries were watching television and having a New Year's Eve party. They didn't know it was our custom to spend New Year's Eve in church. I didn't know why I had to go there, but I went and sat down on a chair and watched TV with them.

Soon they began to pass snacks, but I was so focused on the television that I didn't know who was sitting by me. After a while, I began to feel strange about the girl next to me. She kept serving me over and over, and when she handed me something, I felt a rush of emotions. I had never really spoken English before because no one understood me when I did.

I decided to get up and go, but when I said goodnight, I was talking to this beautiful girl. When I went to tell everyone I was leaving, I found myself addressing her alone as if we had had some kind of plan and I was accountable to her. She was a very attractive young lady, and her face wouldn't go out of my mind. I had been without love for so long that I did not recognize the signs of it.

I left the dining room to go to church. There was no bus to take me, so I walked the whole way, which gave me time to think. As I walked, my heart had no rest from thinking about the most beautiful girl I had ever met.

The problem was that she wasn't from the same culture, and we couldn't communicate because my English was so poor. I never liked to talk to these foreign missionaries. It was so embarrassing when they couldn't understand what I said to them. It was hard for me to hear God saying that she was the one because everything in me was against that idea. I had never been attracted to a white girl before and never thought I would be, but God was taking me into different kind of lifestyle to train me again.

The next day I had to take my little girl, Sifa, to her mom. Everyone at the base was sad about that because she was a sweet girl, and they all loved her. Sifa was sad to go too because she loved many people on the YWAM base—especially a foreign missionary that she always called *Shangazi* (Aunt).

When I was taking her, the girl that I had been attracted to the night before was so sad to see her go. It was then I discovered that this *shangazi* Sifa loved so much was the same girl I was beginning to love. Sifa had to go away, though, because I was getting ready to help lead a team into Burundi and would not have been able to take care of her. Sifa said good-bye to her *shangazi*, and I could see the sadness in this American girl's face.

After I took Sifa to her mother, I came back to the base. The next day, this girl came to me and asked if there was anything she could do to help me keep Sifa there. I knew she wanted to support me in caring for her. I told her, "No, it is not good for Sifa to stay on the base." The truth was that my pride would not let a white girl support this poor black man.

It was a worldview that white missionaries came to Africa with money. Many African people did not get the message of God because their minds were set on receiving money rather than the life-changing word of God. I hated that view, and that could have made me reject her completely. Nevertheless, the way she spoke to me was very nice, and I felt increasingly more attracted to her.

One evening I was tired and needed some entertainment, so I decided to go to the computer room to look at my family reunion pictures. It was about a hundred meters from my bedroom. On the way to the computer room was the dining hall.

There were not many people in the dining hall at that time. But I lost focus and found myself going to the dining hall, instead of the computer room as I had planned. She was there. Bri was her name.

She came out the door when I was coming in. We both stopped.

"Where are you going?" I asked.

"I don't know. Where are you going?"

I told her I was going to look at pictures of my family and asked if she wanted to come with me. She agreed, and we went together as if it was planned, like a date. We looked at the pictures a couple of hours as we talked about different things, like visions and how we were alike or different. This was a good opportunity to talk about ourselves, and neither of us had planned it.

I got tired and told her I was going to bed. However, as we walked each other out, we couldn't separate but continued to talk until we passed the way to her room.

This time I knew something deep was happening inside of us. I asked Bri if she liked me. She looked in my eyes nervously and said that she did. I thought it was too late already, as leaders, to hang out, but I asked her to sit down on a wall outside and talk about ourselves. We talked until around 4:00 a.m.

I broke my limits and views and found myself talking about the possibility and logistics of us getting married. She didn't seem concerned about anything but love. From "Do you like me?" we went to "I think I love you," even though it took a long time that night until we were free and comfortable with each other.

When I got saved, I decided to never get too close to a girl. I was called to preach the Gospel. Moreover, it was impossible to kiss her, but in this time I was soaked in love and wanted to get deeper into it. I was determined to marry her and didn't want to wait, so I kissed her.

I was so excited but also worried. I didn't know how we were able to communicate since I didn't speak English. God works miracles every day in our lives, but how many times do we recognize that? This time I was bold and courageous and speaking good English. We even had a long conversation. After we separated is when I recognized God's miracle.

The previous year I had tried to have a conversation with my teacher in my discipleship school because I had some private questions. When I tried to speak, I lost every word that I thought I knew, and I realized my English needed to be worked on. Since I didn't have money to pay for English lessons, I prayed for God to teach me English Himself.

I was surprised that my English improved so much in one day, and I was able to communicate with my future wife, who spoke not a word of my language. I later remembered how I had prayed and knew that God had answered my prayer.

The next day she came to my door and asked if we could have some time together. I was not sure if she had even slept at all. I was uneasy because the night before seemed so dreamlike. I was not sure whether I had been overcome with emotions or if I had acted from my spirit. It had happened so fast. I wanted more time to pray about it, but she did not have a lot of time. She was returning to Scotland in two weeks.

Her team came from Scotland for two months, and we fell in love the last two weeks they were there, so we didn't have enough time to court. I asked her to not tell anyone until we were very sure. What I didn't know was that she had been praying for me for a while before I knew it.

SURPRISE ENGAGEMENT

A few days before Bri and her team went back to Scotland, we decided to go outside the base to talk about this fast relationship to make sure ours was not just an emotional connection. It was during the rainy season in January. We took the bus, but we didn't have an idea where we were going. I just wanted to get out of the crowd because I am a private person and don't like it when many people are involved in my business.

We left the YWAM base in the afternoon and went to an area called Remera, close to the Kigali International Airport. From there we walked toward the airport because this was the only way to have a private conversation en route with no one else involved.

As we walked to the airport, it began to rain hard, but we focused on what mattered to us the most. We got so wet, but we continued to walk anyway and talk about where this relationship was taking us, asking each other questions

"Do you have someone else in your life that you are considering?" I asked. I had heard that American people get married and divorce very quickly. I had to make sure this American girl was different. In my culture, we don't think of divorce. She told me about the many failed marriages in her family and how she was determined not to get involved in the same mess. I liked that.

She asked me if there were any other girls I was considering for marriage or that I loved. I told her I was still struggling with choosing because I had other girls in my mind, but I hadn't asked them yet. I needed someone who could understand every word I tell her and who could understand things the same way that I did, in the same culture. I wanted to be honest and sure about this intercultural marriage. I had never seen an intercultural marriage in all my family. I had some peace about it but still needed to pray.

She asked me to make a choice: "So do you say, 'Yes, we are engaged,' or no?" This was the hardest thing because I knew if I made the wrong decision, it was going to be a permanent error that could not be removed. Also, if I missed God's guidance, I was going to suffer regret for a long time.

We stopped for a while, and she looked me in the eyes. I still remember her beautiful green eyes staring right into me. I said in my heart, *Well, even if I say yes, and it wasn't God, I will still say she is so beautiful.* Inside I was somehow convinced that she was the one.

I decided and spoke a word that would change my life forever. I said yes. I chose her. Her face was filled with much joy, for God had told her that I was the one for her. We hadn't had any kind of conflict, and I thought it would never happen since she was so smart and such a good listener. Plus she adopted my culture so well that she was praised by every Rwandan who got to see her.

The rain was getting even heavier, so I suggested we go and sit inside the waiting area of the Kigali International Airport. We sat down and enjoyed the warm, dry place and relaxed. We had no more words, but we were just quiet and thoughtful of what was going to happen next.

My spirit was at rest, but my mind needed to be renewed. I was struggling with what I had just done. As I looked around, a security guard came toward me. He looked like he knew us, but I had never seen him before.

I thought he was going to pass, but he stopped and asked me in my language, "Hey, man, are you going to marry this girl, or what are you thinking? You better make no mistake, marry her."

Then he went and came back a bit later after I explained what he had said to Bri, my fiancée. He spoke in English this time. "Okay, I am Christian, and I believe you two are as well. I have a gift of prophecy, so I had to tell you that you guys are a beautiful couple."

That was the first confirmation. I had to decide whether to be bold enough to let everyone know about it or to fear and give up on this unusual situation. We took the bus and went back to the YWAM base. At that time, people were already talking about us and how they saw some kind of relationship going on. However, I asked her to tell no one.

Within a couple of days, her team was all packed and ready to fly back to Scotland, where she had been a missionary for a few years. YWAM Rwanda was so sad to see them leave. As we took pictures and gave hugs to each other, our hugs were longer than any others, and our faces showed almost everything about us. Still I liked to keep very important things private until the right time.

They took the truck and drove away as we waved to them. That made me feel so lonely—more than I had been before we met. I began to worry about her travels and wanted to know how she was doing every minute of the day. She made sure to send me messages when they landed in Kenya and waited for another airplane to Amsterdam. She sent me another when she got to the Glasgow Airport.

As soon as she got to the Paisley YWAM base, she called and told me that they had arrived safely. What joy and loneliness all together!

We talked on the phone a lot in those days. It was during one of our phone conversations the first time a conflict rose up. When I asked her if she kept the secret, she said that she had just told her mother.

"So your whole family knows?" I asked.

"Well just my mom, and I am sure she told my sister too."

I forgot that I had said yes and became angry because she wouldn't keep secrets. She noticed that I wasn't happy about it, and she apologized. I didn't want to talk more.

She began to pray with her leaders, and I did the same thing. I asked my leaders if they thought that it was unusual for a black African man to marry a white American girl. My leader began to tell me about other guys who had good marriages that were mixed also. That encouraged me that I wasn't alone.

Later I decided to tell my brothers, and I called them from the Northern Province where I was on outreach with my team. I only told them that I was engaged, but I didn't tell them what kind of fiancée I had. That itself was another surprise; I had to let them think about one thing at time.

We went to Burundi on outreach, where we preached the gospel in different parts of the country while Bri continued to call me on the phone until we met again.

When we came back from our mission trip, I went to church Sunday morning, thinking about how I was to prepare a wedding without a house or money or even a promise of support. I had nothing except the clothes I had on. My phone sounded right before I entered the church. It was Bri's message: "Honey, we just got done praying for you, and God is going to speak to you the truth today."

I entered the church late, but it was a time of prayer for whoever needed it. I went up front with many other people. Our pastor's wife and other missionary guest speakers were praying for us. After they were done, my pastor's wife continued in tongues with her hand on my head. She began to prophesy over me: "God says you are struggling with love, and He says, 'Love and wait on Him.' You don't have to worry about things. He will take care of it."

I had kept my relationship with Bri a secret. I never told these pastors about it, not even any of their friends. I was surprised, but joyful, because God was in my plan.

Soon Bri went to America and told the news to her whole family with my blessing. She got ready to get married, as we had agreed that we should marry as soon as we could. This was not an easy process while she was in the United States and I was in Africa. We talked only on the phone as we planned the wedding for May of that same year. Like I asked God in my prayer, I needed a fiancée in January and wanted to get married in May or before. This was the most successful prayer in my mission life.

Soon May came, and she arrived at the Kigali International Airport, where I went to meet her with friends and my brothers. It was a joy for her to see other faces in my family, and they teased her in my language. She loved to joke with them and made them laugh. She was a treasure to my family. That made me feel so great, and I began to see myself as a future successful husband.

A CIVIL WEDDING AND MISUNDERSTANDINGS IN RWANDA

In Rwanda, we prepared ourselves for our government wedding on May 24. According to Rwandan culture, we had to have two weddings—one in a government office and another in a church.

The day came, and we got the cars ready. My groomsmen were already there with a nice Cadillac waiting for my bride and bridesmaids. Bri was confused with how things were supposed to happen in my culture because no one had been there to prepare her. I expected her bridesmaids would be with her the whole time of preparation, but they did not show up.

We went to the government office without her maids, and I got angry with them because my plans were interrupted. Even though nobody knew what was going on inside of me, they noticed that I wasn't happy. Bri was very concerned and thought that I was dissatisfied with her. She just wanted to be happy on our wedding day, while I wanted the wedding to go as I planned.

Bri's bridesmaids showed up very late, saying, "On African time." I hated that mind-set and wasn't pleased to see them that late because it sounded as if I failed again. Because my life had been full of too much failure, I was never able to see the signs of success, so I struggled even after the government service as we went to celebrate with family and friends.

We had good food, including our favorite African brochette and fries and drinks. Many people were there taking pictures, but I continued to have the same attitude up to the end of the ceremony.

What I didn't know was what I was doing to Bri. She was all alone in a foreign land on her wedding day with an American expectation of what a wedding is supposed to be like. She expected it to be full of joy and laughter. When the only person she had and the one she depended on the most, her groom, was so unhappy, it crushed her. I didn't learn until later how much that day had traumatized her and planted fears in her that took years to overcome.

After the ceremony and celebration, we went back as a legally married couple, but still not married by the church. We planned to wait almost six months before we were married in the church because we did not have the money for the ceremony.

I wasn't expecting anything wrong to happen because of my attitude, but what happened was the worst for both of us. We went back to the mission base and sat down. I thought we were going to talk about the next step, but Bri was very wounded, and she began to cry.

In my culture, tears mean something big because even women seldom cry. I sat there thinking, "Oh, my Lord, help me. What did I do?"

With strong emotions, she asked why I was so angry at our wedding. She thought I did not want to marry her.

"That is not true," I began to explain, but it seemed too late. I felt even more like a failure.

The conflict was so strong that we both wondered if we had made a mistake. We separated: I went to my room, and she went to hers. As I tried to sleep and rest from the stress, it got even bigger and bigger. I began to think about how we had announced to people that we were a couple and might end up getting divorced the very first day. My whole night went badly and so did hers.

Very early in the morning I decided to restore my relationship with my partner, and I went to her room. I apologized, and she forgave me with more apologies of her own, so we got back together.

I thought that when you get married, everything just works out. I never expected to have conflicts with my wife. Now I know that conflicts and how you deal with them make a marriage stronger.

ADAPTING TO A NEW CULTURE

We started to apply for my UK visa so that we could go to Scotland to continue our mission and have our wedding there instead of waiting six months to be married in a church in Rwanda. We were given a visa very soon, with help of a nice lady at the British embassy who cared about people and their problems.

We were set to fly to Scotland on June 18. We got everything ready, and our friends gave us a ride to the airport in Kigali. I was nervous because it was my first time in an airplane, and I didn't know anything about flights. Soon we were seated in a small airplane that was to take us to Kenya. It was very exciting for me. That first short flight wasn't that bad, and I became more bold as we waited for the next one from Kenya to Amsterdam.

Later, when our flight boarded, we walked onto a much bigger plane. It was an overwhelming experience to be in something so big and beautiful for more than six hours. I couldn't wait to see the Western world with my own eyes. Bri was also impatient to get to her missionary home to show me the beauty of it.

Before we got to Scotland, we had a layover in Amsterdam. It was incredible to see new faces and a new kind of place that I had never imagined. I wanted to touch everything, but I wasn't sure if it was appropriate, so I had to ask Bri.

I was so impatient to get out and see the whole beauty of such a different culture. The people there were so busy; everyone was running, which scared me the most because I wasn't sure if there was something wrong. They spoke different languages and had a different culture, but they seemed so nice and helpful when we interrupted them with questions.

Soon I discovered that it's the culture of much of the Western world to work hard and mind their own business. I also learned that it was not appropriate to watch other people for more than around two seconds, or you may get in trouble for that. I had never heard of staring before as a culturally inappropriate action.

We waited for the next flight for about two more hours and then flew another three hours before we arrived at the Glasgow Airport at around eight in the morning. What an amazing experience, and what a beautiful country! From the airport to our next missionary home, I think everybody thought I was crazy. I was admiring the beauty of the cities, very tall buildings, and nice paved roads everywhere. Even later I noticed that they have paved roads in the forest. I couldn't imagine how blessed the Western world is.

One of the Paisley base staff, John, came to pick us up from the airport in Glasgow. He drove us around the city, and in few minutes, we were home. They called the place Stanely House. (Many of the houses in Scotland are named.) It was a very beautiful tall building with the most beautiful yard I had ever seen. I met the wonderful people there, who gave me an amazing welcome. I felt home already as they showed me what would be my room and everything I needed.

At the end of the tour, Bri took me up on the roof of the house. This became my favorite place because it was a quiet spot to spend time alone with God while I played guitar and sang songs of worship. What a beautiful view it was! You could see the whole city of Paisley and Glasgow.

Bri ran the kitchen at the mission base and I enjoyed cooking with her in their beautiful kitchen. The food they made was so strange to me and I had to learn to follow the health code rules of a British kitchen. They had their way to clean spoons differently than the knives. They had a special sink in the kitchen for washing hands. Everything was done following the rules, and I was scared to break them. It was strange to me, but I loved spending the time with my new wife.

Living this kind of life started to make me feel so uncomfortable. Many times I was in a meeting with staff; most of them were North American missionaries, and a few were Europeans. The only African was me, and I couldn't even understand the topic of their discussion. They would speak very fast. In half an hour, they were done with all subjects and began joking around, while I was still trying to catch up with what they had said from the beginning.

My brain was about to explode, because of pressure of the language and the culture all together. There was no one around who understood my culture.

Western culture seemed to be the opposite of mine, and I felt I would be blamed if I didn't follow. Sometimes I didn't show up to their meetings, especially in the very early mornings, until everybody was concerned about me and asked why I didn't come. I felt like I wasn't part of the mission there, but was helping my wife finish her contract, so that we could leave for good and go back to Rwanda.

She introduced me to her church in Paisley. The people were so kind, as they approached me with a lot of questions in their Scottish accent. It seemed that they didn't realize anyone may not be an English speaker because before I responded to the first question, they would ask the next. I got lost but since their attitude toward me was good, I continued to go there every Sunday.

However, I hated it when Bri stayed late for her social talk, and I had to be involved in those conversations, which of course, was all about her fiancé. Basically the end of service was my test every Sunday. I wanted to go home as soon as the service ended, but their culture demanded we take some tea and biscuits and sit down to get to know each other.

OUR SCOTTISH WEDDING AND "HONEY DAYS"

The leader of our mission base in Paisley was Gary Killingsworth. The next month, on June 25, 2007, we were married by the church. Our pastor was our YWAM leader, Gary Killingsworth, who was the national director in Scotland. This was the number one man that I trusted since he had so much wisdom from God. For that reason he made me feel a little more comfortable to live in a white community. He wasn't just any type of boss; he was a servant leader who worked harder than anyone whom he led. As strong a man as he was, he woke up early and came from his house to start the work at the base before I got up. Sometimes the work was almost done before we joined him.

This was a big challenge to me to see the kind of leader he was as I recounted the leaders in Africa, who wore a suit and tie every day to make sure they looked like leaders. My YWAM leaders in Rwanda were humble like Gary though.

It was Gary that we asked to preside over our church wedding in Scotland. We were married on June 25, 2007. The wedding in Scotland was so different. Bri and I cooked Rwandan food, which was not exactly right because we couldn't find the right ingredients. Everyone had to try it and said it was good, even though I knew it wasn't.

After cooking the meal, I went upstairs and put on the same clothes I wore in my first wedding in the government office. It was a purple shirt and black pants that were both brought to me by Bri from America. She had been given the money to buy my wedding clothes by Connie McKeen, who felt that God had pressed it on her spirit, even though Bri had never asked for such support.

While I was getting dressed, she was downstairs putting on her wedding gown that she had been hiding from me, as her culture required. I discovered that in America, the groom is not supposed to know what the bride will wear in the wedding until the right time.

I came down from my room confused, with no idea what was going to happen, so I joined everyone else in the ceremony hall like it wasn't my wedding. People were smiling at me, and I knew they noticed how lost I was. There were about fifteen people waiting there to witness our marriage ceremony that day. After a little while, my bride showed up with a beautiful white dress and walked down the aisle to where Gary stood. Then I was called to come forward.

Our pastor read the vows and everything else he had to, and then he said, "Now I pronounce you husband and wife." That sounded like the final word we had been waiting for. Then he added, "Kiss your bride." This was not my culture, and I was uncomfortable to kiss Bri in public. Since that was exactly what everyone was waiting to see, I kissed her on the lips in front of them all, and that was the end of the ceremony. Everyone clapped and shouted for joy.

We went to change clothes because we found out that the YWAM staff had paid for a hotel for us to have our honey days. It was three days, which is why we called it our "honey days" instead of a honeymoon.

They gave us a ride to the train station. From there, we traveled by train to Seamill Hotel. Located at the ocean, it was the most beautiful hotel I had ever been in. We got there about seven in the evening, now as a couple before God and man. I was so over-whelmed by the blessings I had and the places God took me. I couldn't believe it was happening so fast, but I had to enjoy eve-rything as if I was used to it.

Our lives began to make sense together as a couple. We didn't have to just see each other in staff meetings, but we stayed together all the time. We had fun playing golf and other games in Seamill in those three days. Then we went back to the base. During that time, I grew more familiar with Bri's accent and speed until I was able to understand most of the words she spoke to me. In times of conflict though, she always won because I couldn't understand a word she said.

We are both thankful to God, who placed us close to the godly couple, Gary and Beverly Killingsworth, who gave us counseling when we needed it. We also had other staff who were so wonderful to us—especially me, who wasn't open to them, yet they were patient with my attitude and reaction when confronted by culture.

Within a couple of months, I was more comfortable, so I asked my wife if there were any ministries in town in which we could participate. She had been working with Teen Challenge and a local soup kitchen, so I joined her there. The first time, I loved what they did, feeding homeless and drug- and alcohol-addicted young adults.

I shared my testimony by the grace of God. Only He could help me communicate with these people because there was no natural way I could understand their questions or that they could understand my English. God is all-powerful, and He worked it all out.

That ministry helped me keep busy and get close to the Lord. I had opportunities to mentor some of the homeless people who thought that no one else understood what they had been through. When I shared my own stories with them, many began to open up their hearts to me and believed in my God, who saved me from genocide and is still saving me today.

I attended a Bible study in the church and hung out with Scottish guys who kept me busy also until December of that year. Just as I was getting used to the Western world, we had to leave and go back to Rwanda. We said good-bye to our friends and YWAM family. It is always sad to say good-bye to YWAMers because you can't find a wonderful community like them anywhere else in the world. We left on December 18, 2007.

BRI'S ADJUSTMENT TO RWANDA

When we got back to Rwanda, we had an amazing experience at the airport. Probably thirty people were there waiting for us—my family, friends, and our YWAM family in Rwanda. They picked us up and took us to our previous missionary base.

As people say, "There is no place like home." I can't even begin to explain the welcome we had there as a couple. It was very joyful for me to return and eat my favorite fresh Rwandan food.

However, it was Bri's turn to learn my culture. People around the neighborhood were never used to her. They just wanted to call her *mzungu* (which means "white person") all the time. Of course she wasn't the only white person around, but most of the locals could not distinguish between her and the other white girls.

This was frustrating to her until she discovered that it wasn't racism. People were friendlier than she thought. She asked me how long she had to live there until they accepted her in our neighborhood and stopped treating her like a foreigner. What she did not understand is that because they could not tell her apart from other white girls, it did not matter how long she was there.

Although people in the neighborhood loved her very much, she was scared to go to the market to buy anything because the Rwandans would charge her two to ten times more than locals, as they do to every white person. That is the ugliest thing to me in my culture. Many people (though not all of them) think of white people as rich but not smart. That is why they charge them too much and expect them to pay what they are told. I struggled with that for a long time, trying to stop people from doing that. But they hated me and sometimes tried to fight me.

People enjoyed calling Bri mzungu as a joke and didn't know they were deeply offending her. Another thing was that, if she gained a few pounds, everybody congratulated her. They intended it as a compliment, but to her, it was an insult.

I suffered rejection from my people, who thought I married Bri because I wanted to be rich. Even her people acted as though they thought the same thing. In the West, people were more cunning in the way they said it, or they never told me at all. I learned what they thought of me through other people. In America, this happens with foreigners who do not fear the Lord, but come and marry local girls to get green cards and then leave them. I have been accused of that. People took account of how long we had been married, trying to judge how much longer I would stay with her.

CHAPTER 11
A VISION OF HOPE

PRAYING FOR AFRICA

In 2007, I was in Scotland with others from various countries in Europe and North America. We all came for the same goal: to serve as missionaries. I was totally different from each of them and had so much experience in misery.

When I arrived in Europe, I realized Africa has a very long way to go, and I started to wonder how we could even start. Every time I prayed, I was convinced that the poverty we have is in our minds first. Other thoughts came to mind that blew my hope away. I kept seeing more and more things that were wrong, and the problem grew bigger and bigger in my mind until it seemed hopeless.

When I thought there was no hope for Africa, I cried out to God. I began weeping inconsolably. Then in the darkness, I lifted my eyes and saw a red light flashing from far on the edge of the city of Glasgow.

I heard a voice in my spirit saying, "Don't cry. Africa is under construction and is flashing, ready to lighten up. She is becoming a light to the whole world, and it's happening right now."

It's amazing how God turns our tears into rejoicing in one instant. When I started to look for news about Africa, I found out that many African leaders were already giving their lives to God. I rejoiced and knew that my vision was from the Lord. Africa is sending many missionaries all over the world. We rejoice at the way God has turned our mess into a big message for all to see.

When God showed me this, it wasn't just for others, but for me also. I lived on the mission for several years and had not even had one supporter, but God provided for me. The problem was that African people didn't care about one of them going to the mission field. Our worldview was that a missionary is a rich white man or woman coming to Africa with money to give to poor people there. With the help of God, Africa is changing, and missionaries are beginning to be sent out from African nations.

It was hard to believe in change for Africa with all that was happening at that time. We had leaders with no interest in the people they led; they were interested in what they could gain from them. There were so many times I needed documents from government offices and saw how hard it was to get service. That makes it hard to pray for those in leadership. The problem is so big you don't even know where to start.

RESISTING CORRUPTION

One time I was asked by the American embassy in Rwanda to go to Kenya while I was applying for a visa to the United States. I went there with my wife, Bri, and daughter, Sifa. We stayed in the Athi River YWAM base between Nairobi and Machakos. We took the bus almost every day to Nairobi, where the American embassy is. The service there was a little intimidating, and the workers were somehow scary.

We were missing one document, so I had to go to Rwanda to get that paper and come back. On our way back to the base, I had to say good-bye to my family and go on alone to Rwanda. As I walked them to their bus, I found out that my passport was gone, along with other electronic items that were with it in my backpack. I called Bri and told her what happened, and we began to pray. It was not easy anymore to get a visa when my passport was stolen.

As I tried to report it to the police, I began to learn how unfaithful the leaders are. First, I didn't know where the police station was, so I took a taxi. The taxi driver charged me a lot of money, and he drove me around the station a couple of times to make me think it was a long drive. Upon our arrival, I paid him with a big bill, which he took, saying he didn't have change. I gave up and went to the police station.

When I spoke to the police officer about my problems, it seemed like he was not listening. He told me to come with him upstairs, and we sat down in a dark room. He asked, "Young man, do you have money?"

"For what?" I asked. I thought this paper was free, but then I thought maybe I had to pay.

I didn't mind having to pay until he said, "Well, how much do you have?"

I asked how much it cost. When he told me that it depended on how much I had, I knew what he meant. This was the way of corruption, and as a Christian, there was no way I was going to pay that money. He told me I was just a kid who didn't know how to deal.

I went downstairs to report the dishonest cop, but this was Kenya. I went to the police officer who appeared to be of the highest rank and told him what happened. He was with other civilians who looked like they were getting robbed also.

He glared at me with red eyes and harshness and said, "If you won't do what he told you to do, get out of the station."

Then I knew that corruption was a stronghold over the whole nation. Later I learned that Kenya is known all over the world as very corrupt. There is a proverb used in Kenya that says, "Even if a goat is tied, it can still help itself to grass." It basically means that they watch out for themselves, no matter what the circumstance.

I went and spent the night at the Athi River base. Early in the morning I woke up and went back to Nairobi to find the Rwandan embassy. There was a lady at the front desk, and I told her everything that happened to me, including my issue with the police.

I was expecting her to be surprised, but she wasn't at all. Instead she said, "Oh, we know them."

It was so relaxing to me to be able to speak to her in my native language. She directed me to another police station in the same building and said to tell them that she sent me. When I told them that I lost my passport and the Rwandan embassy had sent me there, they wrote the report and handed it to me. I discovered then that there was no charge for the document.

I was so proud of Rwanda in that moment for standing above corruption.

The Rwandan embassy couldn't issue or replace passports, so they gave me a paper that would let me cross the borders of Uganda and Rwanda to go back to my country and apply for a new passport. On my way, I was detained for a short time by Kenyan border patrol because I refused again to give them money. They kept the paper and told me that if I didn't pay, they would keep me in jail for a long time.

In the room where they detained me, a few more young men came in who had no identification or passport. I thought that they seemed to know what they were doing though. They paid the border patrol officer about three or five dollars, and he let them go.

That was supposed to be an example for me to do the same. He looked at me and asked, "Did you see that?"

I told him I saw it, but I would not do the same thing because I had a right to pass freely. He got so angry with me and left the room to talk to his boss. They kept me there until the bus that I rode in moved to the Ugandan side of the border.

Then I opened up the door and said to them, "Guys, I don't need your help. I just need my paper now. I have no business with you here."

This time I was angry, and they saw that I was determined. They threw the paper at me and said that I would not pass Ugandan police. I crossed the border of Kenya and Uganda and went to the bus, while everyone else was supposed to show their passport to the Ugandan police. I knew the Ugandan police could be even worse, so I kept my paper until I crossed the border of Uganda to Rwanda. I felt like a big cloud lifted over my head. It was so good to be home.

I showed the border police in Rwanda the paper. He asked me why there was no stamp from any Kenyan or Ugandan border patrol.

When I was just beginning to explain, he stamped it and said, "I know." Then I knew there was a big difference between Rwanda and other African nations, and I was proud to be Rwandan.

I still have hope for all of Africa. Although it seems to me that Rwanda seems so much less corrupt than other African nations, I know that we still have more growing to do as well. I believe that God is working in Africa and we will see great change as our leaders turn to Him. Every journey starts with a small step and I rejoice at the steps I see Africa taking.

CHAPTER 12
A GREAT PROMISE

MY SONG OF HOPE

"Ask and it will be given to you, seek and you will find, knock and the door will be opened to you" (Matthew 7:7).

In April of 1994, Rwanda was in the crisis of genocide. It was a horror like this world had never seen before—not by the number of people killed, but by the number of killers. Normal, every day people became bloodthirsty executioners. Neighbors killed neighbors; friends killed friends; husbands killed their own wives and children. Pastors and religious leaders lured thousands to their deaths with false promises of security.

Some people cannot comprehend what happened; it seems like far-off stories of fiction. But I was there, and I saw it all. The great nations of the world weren't asleep; they were watching. Some of them were even involved in the slaughter of innocent people.

I never knew anything my parents had done to deserve death, but people came and attacked us, intending to kill us all. We tried to run, but there was no place to go. I no longer knew what was true and whom to trust. My former teachers and the parents of my friends now hunted us like animals. I didn't know who was Tutsi and who was Hutu. All I knew was the death that consumed my world and choked out any hope or sanity within me.

Our entire government was unified for the destruction of one minority tribe. For some time, Tutsi had been prohibited from

holding government positions or even pursuing higher education. This meant we were not equipped to resist when the Hutu
leaders turned against us.

Before the genocide, my brother, Shyaka, was a businessman
who was successful in the village. He was one of a few people
able to afford a nice cassette radio. He loved worship and gospel
songs, and he bought with the radio a tape of one of the famous
choirs in Kigali. It was the new album of a Pentecostal church
choir called Hoziana. It was their song from Matthew 7:7 that
had stuck in my head throughout the genocide and had become
my prayer.

> You promised if we ask,
> It will be given to us;
> And if we knock,
> The door will be opened to us.

This is the only part of the song that I remembered. As I ran,
I sang this part unconsciously, but then when I took cover somewhere, I had to ask my heart what it meant. This was the song of
promise that never left me.

I was an unbeliever, who was trying to find a solution to his
trials without a clue regarding who would help. I questioned
myself, "What am I singing, and why is this song not going away?
What does it mean?"

I had heard of God before. I was a member of the Catholic
church and attended services very often, but I had never heard
of salvation before. I didn't know why we went to church, but I
knew how fun it was.

I also remember the preachers who came to town often, but
we didn't care about what they said. Instead, we went to watch
the movies they sometimes showed on projectors. That was a big
deal in town because before the genocide I had never watched
movies or knew anyone who owned a TV.

Not too long before the genocide, I had heard the song by the Hoziana choir that stuck in my head. Before our horrors began, God used many people in the way of prophecy, but our stubborn minds did not receive their message. There was even a man in my own village who spoke about the impending killings, but we thought he was crazy, and no one listened to him. Even though we did not understand what we heard, I can assure you that our brains kept some messages. The Hoziana choir was one of those prophets of the time.

Many times I was caught in the traps of the killers and was almost destroyed, but the song kept ringing in my ears, as if the radio was with me.

MISPLACED VALUES

The saying "Ask and you shall receive" isn't a joke. We may just be poor-minded and take it lightly, never knowing how powerful the word of God is. God delights to give us all that He has purposed for us. He delights to give us miracles, healings, wisdom, the salvation of our families and neighbors, and immeasurably more than we could imagine. That is what God says in the Bible.

I have found that we spend a very long time asking for money, while we really don't need it. It's just the love of money that grows within us, which is dangerous for anyone who seeks to serve the Lord. Most often we desire money for things that we do not need. God is faithful to meet our needs; it is our wants that get us into trouble. The love of money can cause people to be so desperate to have it; they act as if they have none, even when they are well provided for.

When Jesus was about to be crucified, there was preparation that needed to be done, and a woman was chosen to do it. As we read in Matthew 26:6–13, Mark 14:3–9, and John 12:1–8, Mary, the sister of Lazarus, went to the place where Jesus was having dinner with His disciples and friends. She pulled out a bottle of expensive perfume and poured it all onto Jesus. However, Judas was greatly offended at this because of his love of money.

Judas thought, *What a waste!* His excuse was that, if they sold this perfume, they would get a lot of money to help the poor. Honestly though, he had been stealing from the money bag (John 12:6). His greed blinded his vision so he could not see the beautiful act that Mary was performing out of love for Jesus.

In the genocide, a couple that lived near us kept money in their house during the killings. As I grew up, this couple with their three children lived the same lifestyle as anyone else—I mean a very average life. They had many hundreds of cows, and they never bought anything of value more than others in the village. Their son told me that someone tried to help them to go to Burundi before this terrible thing happened. The parents refused to do what would have saved their lives because they thought it was a waste of money.

During the genocide, the family members were all killed, except the youngest son. When they found his mom where she was hiding, she had so much money—more than anyone else in that village. The killers talked about it for a long time, and they rejoiced. The money she had with her was enough to save hundreds of people, if they had taken action before this situation started. Today we have more people like that who will even die for their money or to get more money.

FAULTY PRAYERS

In my early Christian life I struggled in my prayers. I found myself focusing on money instead of what I really needed. I felt disappointed many times, when my prayers were not answered. I never prayed a wrong prayer when I was in trouble or in big danger.

I have found that, in times of peace, people get distracted by many things. When they pray, they say whatever comes out of their mouths without thinking. This is when we hear people praying as if they are victims or the only ones suffering. Sometimes I hear people questioning why God did this or that as if they are accusing Him of evil deeds. They ask, "Why did God let this happen to me?" We hear them complain, but never once do they give thanks for any good He has done in their lives.

Growing up in the Catholic church, I knew how to pray the church prayers, such as the Hail Mary. Our services always ended with the Lord's Prayer. That was all I memorized, but I didn't know the meaning of those prayers. I didn't say any prayers of my own, so then I think I never really prayed before.

There comes a moment when you know what to pray for because the time you have is too short to complain or play around. One time I was in a situation that I had to know how to pray because all these general prayers would not work for me. I recognized the needs of both my body and soul. There was not a preacher to teach me how; neither was anyone around who had a prayer that I could repeat. We were all desperate, with no one to give us hope. But eternity is put into the hearts of men (Ecclesiastes 3:11), and God is always ready to reveal Himself when we seek Him.

No one can know how to pray unless they have revelation from the Holy Spirit. And the Holy Spirit never comes to you when you ignore Him. The key is to give your whole life to Jesus, and then he will send you His Spirit.

There I was, a religious young man who had not a clue whether God was real, but God was trying to reach out to me and show me who He is. He is the God who can do the impossible and change the unchangeable. I had to meet Him personally so that when I tell people who He is, I won't tell them out of my theology or wisdom of man. He is God above all, that is how I know Him.

There was a time I said, "God, I know this may be too hard for You, and I understand that, but please can you take me to heaven after they kill me?" God had to show me that there is nothing impossible for Him.

There is a game I used to play with my family. We would be given clues, and then we would have to guess what the leader of the game was thinking. This is how God helped me to know how to pray. He knows that my brain couldn't find out by itself, so He created a spiritual environment to give me a clue, through the radio and the cassette that played at the right time.

So I asked God a question, "Can this promise apply to me now?"

"Ask and you shall receive," the answer came.

But remember that I didn't know who said it. I didn't know it was in the Bible. I didn't even know what the Bible held inside because I had never opened it before.

God had already planted a seed in me before anything happened even though I ignored it. It was there, even when I made fun of God's people and insulted them. The seed was being planted in me. There were many times that I saw men and women carrying Bibles in their hands, but I thought they had some problem in their brains. They sang to Jesus and preached about Him. Even though they sounded like a bell ringing behind the mountain, that planted a seed that someday I would wonder about. That made me think God must exist—I mean a real, powerful God.

Prayer is supposed to be a special relationship with God that leads a person to ask Him for the things He delights to give us. It is a time to commune with God. Even though He already knows what we need, He wants us to ask in order to build a relationship with Him.

I learned this from my daughter, Sifa, when she came to live with me at the age of six. She was staying with me at the YWAM mission base in Rwanda. Even though I knew that her mom was a Christian, I wanted to teach her about God. So every night, I would ask her to pray before she went to bed. My wife and I were so excited to have this precious life to train up for God's purpose. We prayed together taking turns: I went first, then Bri, and then Sifa.

The first night I was so impressed at how a very young girl could pray such hard traditional words like an old person. She prayed in Kinyarwanda, and Bri asked me what Sifa had said because she seemed so serious, like a little prayer warrior. It was unusual for a six-year-old child to pray such a long, serious prayer.

Her prayer went something like this: "God, the Father of our Lord Jesus Christ, the Rock of Ages, above all the nations, please protect us tonight."

Some of the words were so traditional and were not even used in our lifetime. I was very interested in the wisdom of such a little girl.

The next night, Bri and I were so excited to hear her pray again. We prayed in turn, and Sifa again prayed a very traditional prayer with big words. Bri asked what Sifa had prayed this time, and it was hard for me to translate word for word. It was as if she spoke in "King James English."

The third night, when Sifa prayed the same prayer again, I was concerned. I asked her what "Rock of Ages" meant. She acted like she had never heard these words before. I explained to her that those were the words she was praying every night and asked her who had taught her that prayer. She said that she did not know; it was just how she always prayed. She shrugged her shoulders and turned the palms of her hands up defensively, like she thought she was in trouble.

It sounded so familiar to me because I attended the same church that her mom did. I had heard such words at prayer meetings in her mother's denomination. They spoke this way—not only in their prayers, but in their songs, old and new. Later I told Bri that Sifa had copied her prayer from her mom. Now we wanted to train her to pray from her heart, not from memory, where she saved her religious phrases.

I would wait for my daughter's turn to pray and ask her to not repeat any of the words she usually said. She slowed down and ran out of words. Then I knew she was not really praying, but reciting a phrase she had memorized. I was the same way before I met the Holy Spirit. So is every one else, who repeats the same words every day, instead of speaking what God lays on their hearts.

This little girl had grown up in a Christian community. She was intimidated by settings in which everyone prayed aloud. Without knowing why, she defended herself by copying her mom's prayer. So whenever she was asked to pray, she would impress people with her sophisticated language.

There are different things that may influence the way we pray. Many copy friends, elders, or pastors. As I travel, I see people in various churches act exactly like their pastors or other spiritual leaders, which is sometimes very good. The danger is that a person may never submit to the leading of the Holy Spirit but will stand on their own spiritually.

The religious system teaches us how to pray and what to pray, and then we wonder why God does not answer our prayers. Many churches have written out their prayers so people can memorize them. They are taught to recite one of these whenever they need something.

Allowing God to guide your prayers brings you closer to His heart. I still remember almost every prayer that changed my life, even before I met the Lord. When I got involved in religious activities and began to hear others praying, I thought they were so impressive and smarter than me in their prayers. I thought I needed to learn from them.

We speak so many words every day and never stop to think of what we are saying. How can God answer you according to your prayers when you don't even remember what you asked? If you really pray, you never forget what you said, and that will be your testimony. "You do not have because you do not ask God" (James 4:2c).

CHAPTER 13
THE ZEAL TO REACH OUT

SHARING WITH FRIENDS

The culture in America is so different than the culture in which I grew up. I found it so hard to witness to others about Christ. In America, it seemed everyone claimed to be a Christian but wanted nothing to do with Jesus. All I said appeared to fall on deaf ears, and I often found myself very discouraged.

Every time I think about poverty, I think of those unreached by the gospel of Jesus. Everyone I led to Christ seemed to begin to prosper in some way. Not all of them became rich, but their lives were changed.

When I got saved, I was so excited to reach out to my friends, whom I loved so much. I realized that, if they didn't get saved, they would end up in hell. What a loss! It became my first passion to make sure my friends were safe.

My prayers were mostly answered. When I prayed, I was often prompted to act, as well. It's for that reason I decided to go to each one of them, after I prayed and fasted, to tell them the Good News. It was those that God had led me to witness to that He brought to my mind in the times I needed it most.

One friend of mine that God laid on my heart was Elvis, one of the two that had joined me in the bush at Saint Andre after our failures to pray. We were close friends, and before I got saved, I spent most of my time at his house drinking and talking. He worked for his sister, who owned a restaurant-bar, and he always welcomed me with a bottle of Mutzig, which was our favorite beer. We drank and drank until we got too drunk, and then we separated.

After I was saved, I went to visit Elvis again. This time I was a different person. I didn't know whether he was going to accept the change I had made or if I was going to see the end of our friendship and make a new enemy. Many times when I approached my old friends with the gospel, they would become angry and not want anything else to do with me. I had confidence with Elvis, though. I took a bus and went to his sister's restaurant, where I usually found him working.

It had been almost three years since we had seen each other, and when he first saw me, he was so surprised. After a very long warm welcome, as was always his way, he gave me the same chair on the front porch where we always sat. Then he ran inside and grabbed a bottle of beer.

"Well, my friend, you will have to forgive me, but I am not going to drink beer," I told him.

His arms dropped in discouragement, and he began to question me, "Are you kidding? This is not like you. What's wrong, man?"

"Brother, this is a long story. We have to talk."

He sat down and started to guess. "Did you become like those crazy Christians?"

It was if I could read his mind, but he couldn't understand my language anymore. I started to tell him my story from the day we had separated, after we got kicked out of school. I told him of the failures and struggles I had been through and how I questioned if God was real. He really focused on me, and the conversation got very serious. Even though I had confidence, I was still nervous to share my faith with him, for fear that I would lose him as a friend.

As I told him about my discovery at Rilima, he was extremely touched by the whole story. He had nothing else to add to it. He was always a man of few words, but this time he was almost mute. I couldn't get him talk.

He looked at me as if I was an alien. Then Elvis said, "Man, if you can become a believer, I will also."

Obviously, the change from the kind of person I was before I met Jesus to who I became after my conversion was enough to convince others of the truth in my story. No one believed I could get saved. I was always a troublemaker.

When Elvis learned that my life changed, he was ready to change his too. We prayed together, and the beer he opened for me was the last he drank. Today he is still a follower of Christ. He is a very good businessman and owns his own shop. Every time we meet, he never stops telling me how God blessed him and how the wisdom of God has guided him.

FAITH PUT TO THE TEST

In 2002, there was a time that, without really knowing what I was requesting, I asked God to try my faith. It was after I heard many stories of men and women of God who prayed for the sick and saw them healed. They even saw blind eyes opened and the dead raised. I was so hungry for more faith in Jesus so that I could glorify God.

I often asked those who were more mature in the faith how others could see the sick healed but not us. The answer was always, "Go ask God to use you." I was willing to pay the price and do whatever it took to have that kind of faith.

It was for that reason I prayed, "God, if faith is free, I am asking for all of it, not a fraction. If there is a price to pay, I am ready to pay it."

I asked God to give me a challenge to see if I really got the faith I desired. I boldly asked, without knowing what it was that God could possibly allow me to go through. Surely it would be nothing like anything I had expected. I thought that maybe it would be praying for blind eyes to be opened, but I hoped that it would not be in public because if it didn't work, it would be embarrassing. I was the one that was blindsided by what that test turned out to be.

I left Rilima around 5:00 p.m., trying to catch a bus. I was too late, for all the vehicles were gone. As I stood on the road thinking about how I could get a ride, I heard a truck rolling by. It was carrying a lot of baggage in the back. Since I needed to get to town, I lifted my hand, signaling for ride.

What I didn't know is that I was asking for a ride on a death truck. Carefully pulling over, the driver seemed to be in good communication with his escorts in the back of the truck, who wore the government uniform of the local defense. Although they were in uniform, I didn't know if they actually were officers. I didn't care at first; I just needed a ride home.

I jumped in the truck bed and enjoyed the crazy ride down a muddy road on top of bags of potatoes and many other kinds of goods. As I sat with these very dark-skinned, tall, muscular guys, about five of them kept their eyes on me, as if I was about to jump out of the truck.

They continuously asked me the same question, "Where are you going again?"

I repeated, "Kigali town." This began to make me a little nervous, but I kept thinking positively.

In about two hours, we were in a town where I hadn't been before, and they stopped. They had other connections in a place that looked like an open-air market. At this time, it was dark, and there was no electricity in town. Everything turned darker and darker. They huddled together. They were whispering like I wasn't even there. I understood then that I had been kidnapped.

These types of killings were common after the genocide. It happened years later to one of the other survivors that I ran with during the killings in my village. He was attacked in 2007 when he wanted to go and visit the place where his parents' house used to be. It was Sunday morning around 9:00 a.m. Before he reached his destination, he had to pass through the houses of the released prisoners, who more than likely killed some of his family in the genocide.

Many of killers were released from prison after they confessed their crimes and asked the government to have mercy on them. The incredible number of killers in the genocide made it impractical for the government to keep them all imprisoned. Instead, they sought reconciliation between the Hutu and Tutsi tribes. Showing mercy to the killers was an attempt to bridge a large gap. Thousands were released without their captors really knowing whether their repentance was genuine.

As soon they spotted this young man, the Hutus ran toward him with their machetes and cut him into pieces. It was overwhelming for the survivors of the genocide to have endured such horrors, only to see their families picked off one by one later. Some of them couldn't take it anymore and retaliated one night in a surprise attack. The next morning, they themselves were arrested and put into prison.

It was in the atmosphere of those secret killings that I found myself that year. I was kidnapped by a group of men who were involved in the genocide but were placed in positions of local security because they had been members of the army.

Many soldiers from the former army were retrained in an attempt to unite them with the RPF. They were told that Rwanda had to be united, and they were taught that the tribal groups were lies and underwent much training to transform their minds that had been consumed with so much evil.

What actually happened, though, is that many underwent the training just to be put into positions where they could continue the killing they had begun. While Rwandans inside the country struggled to rebuild the nation, leaders of the genocide outside our borders continued to influence those within to stay true to their original aim.

Those recruited soldiers were ready to eat me alive. I had no phone. Even if I had, there was no one to call to come to my defense. So I prepared myself, knowing that I was alone in my battle. It was then that I remember the prayer I had prayed months before, asking God to give me complete faith and to test me.

I remembered who God was. I remembered that miracles were not difficult for Him, but all he had to do was speak, and the world was created. I felt so much joy in my heart, knowing that God was watching over me.

Their plan was for the driver to leave me stranded there, with the armed security officers and other civilians that were united with them. Night had fallen, and it was hard to see more than five meters in front of me. The driver jumped back into the cab, while one of the security officers who looked like the devil himself jumped into the back. When I tried to climb onto the truck as well, he swung his Kalashnikov rifle at me and almost hit me.

"You can't leave me here. I came with you," I pleaded.

The driver stuck his head out the window and signaled to the officers who were left with me, "Hey, guys, take care of that boy."

His meaning was clear. I walked behind the truck, which took off like a flash of lightning and was gone.

It wasn't easy for them to catch me in the dark, but they tried. Because I couldn't see either, I knew that if I ran, I could fall and be easily overtaken by them. I moved away slowly, remembering that my father had told me to walk slowly and pay attention to your surroundings when you are in the middle of an attack. He told me to listen to where the sound of shooting or marching was coming from.

I was soon cut off by two of them. They stood in front of me, but they did not touch me.

"I think this is him," one said to the other. The other one suggested that they call the rest of their group.

My heart stayed at peace, thinking, *God, how can You trust me so much that You trust me with this test?* I began to pray. I knew in my heart that God was testing me and it wasn't my battle to fight.

I waited patiently, and they decided to go tell the others that they had found me. I couldn't understand why they didn't just attack me. Was I a great big man to them, or did I look like a lion in front of them? I didn't understand, but I trusted God.

When they left, I almost laughed out loud, but I kept quiet. I was full of joy and worry at the same time. I could not believe these two guys with big muscles and guns in their hands didn't think they could catch a skinny guy like me. I probably weighed 120 pounds then. I forgot that I knew karate, for I was more interested in God's protection of me.

I walked away until I met a boy who was standing there on the street. I asked him the name of the town. I asked if there were any military headquarters close. He mentioned Gako, which was probably fifty miles away. I felt hungry, so I asked about a restaurant, and he walked me to a restaurant that sold bread and tea.

As soon as we walked in, I spotted the security officers that had kidnapped me. They were talking about how I had escaped them.

My prayers began to ascend like I was shooting at heaven with a gun. I can't even think of what I prayed.

They actually looked afraid, with their guns on their laps.

I ordered some bread and walked out with the boy. Fear coursed through my veins, and I asked the boy to walk faster. He knew something was wrong, and after we walked about a hundred meters, he stopped.

"What's wrong, man? Why did you stop?" I asked.

"Knock at this door. They will open for you. They are the best people I can think of in this town." He point at a house with a wooden door and a dark front porch.

When I looked in his eyes, I knew he was serious. Before I knocked twice, the door opened, faster than I thought. It was as if they had been waiting for me. A man in his forties looked all around me to make sure I was alone.

"How can I help you?" he asked.

"I am running from the local security guys, who have guns and I think…"

Before I finished, he pulled me inside. "We know. Come in."

Inside I saw a table prepared for dinner with nice cassava bread and vegetables. His pregnant wife sat at the table quietly. The man disappeared into the back of the house, and in a few seconds returned with a gallon of warm, fresh milk.

"*Karibu*," the man told me. (It means "Welcome" in Swahili.) He introduced his wife and himself to me. He told me he was a pastor in that area at a Pentecostal church. I wanted to believe that he was a good man because of what the boy had told me, but I couldn't forget what had happened in the Pentecostal church during the genocide. I didn't know if he was a different kind of pastor.

Although I was still guarded, I introduced myself and explained what had just happened. He told me not to worry and that he would get me a ride home in the morning.

Soon after we ate, they laid a very comfortable mattress on the floor right there in the living room. I became more confident that this couple might be instruments of the Lord placed there for me. I slept soundly that night, and morning came quickly. It was early the next morning, probably around five, when I heard the pastor walk out the door. I waited a bit nervously to see what he was up to.

About ten minutes later, he returned to wake me up. "Hey, are you still sleeping? Didn't I tell I would get you home early? Get up. Your ride is here."

I couldn't believe that after being kidnapped, I was actually going to make it home early. There was another truck that looked like the first one, but the driver was different. This time I sat in the front seat.

We left after I blessed the pastor and his family. They had been so kind to me, and I now believed for sure that they were the best people in town. Not too far down the road, the driver turned on the radio, and we began to worship with beautiful Kinyarwanda music until we got to town. I blessed the driver and his friends, and then I left, knowing that I had seen my miracle.

I knew God had answered my prayer for faith. I was filled with joy and hope for the future.

As safe as Rwanda is today, you can't imagine such a thing happening. I have witnessed such amazing forgiveness that I think we Rwandans could become one of the most powerful nations on earth. It was prophesied to us that God is going to make us a light to the whole world. I was so focused on that promise that I never thought that there were still some people who were not happy with the peace we now have. I still believe the prophecy, but I also think my eyes were opened by this experience, and I know that the enemy of our souls is still preparing traps for us.

CHAPTER 14
SIN DEVELOPMENT

THE SEEDS OF HATRED

Growing up in Rwanda has taught me so much about how sin and hatred evolve. Long before I was born, people began to separate themselves into groups according to social status, and then the groups were given names. Later, when Rwanda was colonized, the two groups were permanently separated. Before, a person could move from one group to another, but at the time of colonization the divisions became rigid. The country that colonized Rwanda took individuals and put them into each group according to height, broadness of their noses, the number of cows they owned, intelligence and many other qualities. The elite were called Tutsi, while the less impressive majority were called Hutu. The devil waited for his seed to grow for many years.

It did not take long for resentment to grow among the Hutu. Soon an unspoken hatred for Tutsi grew in Rwanda. This hatred intensified until it became violent and murderous. Eventually the majority of the Hutu in Rwanda were convinced that killing all Tutsis would be the answer to the life they desired.

When I was growing up, I was somehow shielded from the hate that surrounded me. Sometimes in school we would be asked to identify ourselves as Hutu or Tutsi, and I was not sure what I was. My parents did not talk about it. Sometimes I would say that I was Hutu; other times I would say that I was Tutsi.

I didn't understand the truth because of my youth, but there was much going on. Western countries claimed that they could not have foreseen that genocide would occur, but those who lived in Rwanda knew it would happen. Many of us did not comprehend the fullness of the situation until we were old enough to make our own way. Very few Tutsis had a chance to go to a higher level school. As we began to attempt any kind of business or higher education, doors that had been slammed shut decades before remained tightly sealed.

As I got older, I began to understand more. People were being killed in secret, and the hate propaganda became increasingly more frequent and adamant about the death of all Tutsis. We lived in fear, waiting for the day we would be attacked.

I don't know how long we will hide these seeds of hatred between Hutu and Tutsi. This hatred has continued until today. I am sure that there are Hutus that I may encounter in other countries that would kill me because I was born a Tutsi. Hatred does not end because a war is over or because a government has made laws against it.

Words have power. They are heavy enough to weigh a person down. In many cases, words endure long after years and people pass away. Over the years, words were spoken between Hutu and Tutsi that, little by little, created a great divide that is only repairable by an almighty God. Since we never forgot any single word we had spoken between Hutu and Tutsi, this caused a lot of bitterness in our lives that is still stirring up resentment inside many today.

The potential for evil is in all of us. Who knows what is being built around the world today? I hear people making jokes about race, regions, religions, and so on. It is taken lightly, but the lasting effect of such things is often unseen until it reaches to a breaking point. From bullies and cliques in the schoolyard, to gossip and envy in the church, seeds of bitterness and hatred are constantly being sown.

The genocide in Rwanda was an example of what feeding hatred looks like on a large scale. It was not necessarily the number of Tutsi that were killed that made it so horrific, but the number of Hutu that committed torture and murder. Many of the individuals involved in these depraved, gruesome acts would have been considered "good people" before the war began.

There is a battle that has been waged over our minds and spirits. Too often, we allow unholy thoughts to reside within our minds because we feel that it is "normal" to do so. The Bible tells us otherwise:

> Finally, brothers and sisters, whatever is true, whatever is noble, whatever is right, whatever is pure, whatever is lovely, whatever is admirable—if anything is excellent or praiseworthy—think about such things.
>
> —Philippians 4:8

I challenge you now to take stock of what thoughts you entertain and what attitudes you allow to take up residency within you. What may seem like a small thing to us can grow until it consumes us.

You never know who planted the seeds of thoughts you are entertaining today. We need to recognize that what we may see as harmless is actually a seed of evil that we give ground to.

Every word spoken to a Mexican in America or to a white man in China or to a Chinese in Africa is still battling in their minds, as long as it takes to grow the seed the devil has planted. We choose what to do with the words that have been spoken to us and what seeds we plant in others. I tell you the truth, one of these days, every one of us is going to be judged or justified by every single word we have spoken.

Living in America, I have observed a lot of prejudice and ill words spoken over nationality and ethnicity. Probably because there are so many different people from different backgrounds, there is a lot of opportunity for judgment of those that are differ-

ent. Unfortunately, some of the greatest prejudice I have seen is among those that are countrymen.

One sad point of separation I noticed is between blacks and whites. We make jokes about it and smile. No one likes to talk about it, but the hurts and resentment often run deep in our hearts. Acts of violence and anger often reveal what has festered under the surface. African people blame white people for coming and making them slaves, dividing them into groups, killing them and attacking with an onslaught of other grievances. Some of these things may have occurred centuries before, but we need to uproot them before these destructive attitudes grow too deep.

People say that it is no longer an issue, but I have witnessed for myself how real racism is in America today. A lot of white people unconsciously stereotype blacks, and blacks unconsciously stereotype whites. Whenever I hear things like this, I take it so seriously because I know how it all starts and where it can lead.

We are then faced with the question of what to do about it. Should we move on and ignore it, or cut it off and uproot the evil among us?

My whole life I watched people pretend that nothing was wrong. The result in Rwanda should serve as a lesson to the whole world. It can be as simple as a few people forming a group called Hutu and Tutsi or Twa. It can be as simple as calling someone upper class or lower class, Northern or Southern, trailer trash, snob or redneck.

THE FIRST STEP TO CHANGE

It doesn't matter how far back discrimination began. The truth is, at some point, someone needs to be humble, courageous, and loving enough to start the process of reconciliation. Our problem is not that we created racial tensions; the problem is that we never ask for forgiveness and put an end to it. If someone started the conflict, someone needs to start a reconciliation process.

Martin Luther King Jr. and many others started a journey of freedom. We need to continue this work with reconciliation. There can be no true freedom without reconciliation.

Although there have been many monumental cases of reconciliation in Rwanda between Hutu and Tutsi, we still have a long way to go before the nation is healed completely. We are still in need of reconciliation. Many Tutsi still hang onto the wrong that was done to them, or they remain stubborn, claiming that the first step of reconciliation has to come from the Hutu in repentance. I have heard many Hutu refusing to repent, saying, "Tutsi killed Hutu as well. They have to repent."

I think of Daniel praying for his people: As righteous as he was, he stood before God, repenting for what he had not done, confessing all the sins of Israel, putting it all on himself. If you are in need of reconciliation, look at your side first. Even if the other person is 99 percent responsible for the offense, repent for your one percent. When you make the first step, God is faithful to reward your humility and love. Even if the other person never repents, you stand before God unburdened and free because you have done your part.

Repent as you confess your wrong doing or wrong motives. This will bring forgiveness and clear the path for healing. Many times, when a person is approached in humility, love, and a true heart of repentance, their natural reaction is to respond in like manner.

If you go to the other person with accusations, it will bring past offenses alive again and reopen deep wounds. Accusations often escalate the situation, and the pain and anger become as strong as they ever were, if not stronger. The answer will never be found in accusations.

This is the case in Rwanda. It is true that many Hutu were killed, although the number is far, far less than how many Tutsi were killed. Some Hutu that did not support the killing of the Tutsi were murdered at the hands of the killers. Some Hutu were killed in defensive fighting at the hands of Tutsi. Many Hutu were killed in battle against the RPF, and unfortunately there were innocent Hutu that were killed in retaliation by civilians and RPF soldiers alike. This was highly discouraged by the RPF however, and those responsible for retaliation killings were often brought to swift justice and sometimes executed by the RPF.

The reason it was called genocide of the Tutsi is that detailed plans were carried out with great care in an attempt to completely erase the existence of Tutsi from the face of the earth—along with any Hutu who defended them. It was an attack decades in the planning. Radio broadcasts that called Hutu civilians to take up arms and exterminate the "Tutsi Cockroaches" clearly show that it was premeditated and fueled by hatred.

Unfortunately, those who died were not the masterminds of the slaughter, but those that had been brainwashed into defending an evil cause. Some of those responsible have been brought to justice, but many are still in hiding, plotting their next attack. Some have even been bold enough to go public, calling for the repentance of Tutsis in an attempt to excuse their crimes. This is one of the biggest mistakes you can make if you are looking for reconciliation.

I mourn for the lost lives of Hutu soldiers who thought they were fighting for a noble cause, but I rejoice in the victory of the RPF. It was the RPF alone who ended the genocide. Their victory brought peace. I have yet to see a war that has been stopped without casualties.

Many criticized Kagame for taking as long as he did to stop the war. Many say that he could have saved many, many more Tutsi if he had moved his troops faster instead of focusing on military strategy. For sure, all of those who worked for peace in Rwanda could be criticized—from Kagame to the United Nations to foreign powers—but placing blame will do nothing to heal our country or undo what has been done.

In America, I can still see a divide between many black and white Americans. White Americans have done horrendous things to their black countrymen. But unfortunately, it has gone the other way too. How beautiful it would be if black Americans truly followed the heart of Martin Luther King Jr. and acted in love toward their former oppressors, taking the first step of reconciliation. Even though the divide was not originally created by them, they can stand up and repent for any unloving acts that were committed on their side. Many believe that the white Americans should be the first ones to make such a move, but the Bible tells us that the last shall be first.

It does not matter who wronged whom first; what matters is shall be the first to act in love. There have been many heroes in the world who have set this example. Martin Luther King, Abraham Lincoln, and Nelson Mandela are just a few wise men from whose actions can learn.

Whatever name we put on our cause, we must be active in our fight against the evils of this world. Run to receive the prize.

WHOSE CHURCH IS IT?

The view of the world prevails even in our churches. A church is not one man's business. For God to dwell among His people, the Holy Spirit needs to be the leader of all. Too often, the "houses of God" have become the possession of the people, and no one else has liberty to fellowship with illumination from the Holy Spirit. In our world today, too many services are planned on a computer, and there is a program for the year. If the Holy Spirit wanted to use someone, the church leaders might be angry.

After the genocide in Rwanda, we had tribal churches, but no one could admit it. We all claimed Jesus was our Lord and Savior, but if you went to a different church, they would recognize you and be careful with you. They would judge you according to your nose, your height, your clothes, etc.

Praise God, I've seen some changes. Many leaders were found guilty of being involved in the genocide, even though they were still teaching about Jesus. They would never let anyone say anything from the Holy Spirit because they were afraid of the truth. Here is where the sin really develops faster and stronger. After killing, you go to preach to hide your crime. After fornication, there comes an abortion to make sure nobody will know.

Another time I was leading an evangelism team in Rwanda to a big church, with a choir and speakers. The whole time, the Holy Spirit pressed me to speak. Before I started, one of the leaders pulled me aside.

"Theo, I know you sometimes are so bold when you speak, but today I want to advise you," he began. Then he started to tell me all the things a pastor never says, so I could be careful. Everything he told me not to say was my subject to speak about.

My response was, "You know what? Let's pray and ask the Holy Spirit to lead me." We prayed, and I spoke the truth that the Lord had revealed to me, unafraid of man and his judgment. I spoke with no caution. I could see one part of the church was surprised but happy with me, and the other part was angry.

What we hide may be the tool to destroy us in the future. Sin spreads like a virus in our bodies. It always starts with a little thought in our minds. If you recall what our first parents did, it was as simple as eating a fruit.

Now take a look at this world we live in today. It is confusing because sin has become so much a part of our lives that we don't even recognize it as sin anymore. We find ourselves trying to figure out what sin is. It's become our habit and so much a part of our culture that we can't even tell it's wrong anymore. To be a vessel that is fully given to the Lord, we have to die to ourselves. A large part of this may be rejecting the culture that shaped us.

From the very beginning, God first created Adam, then Eve. Right away the devil began his work through Eve to Adam. When they chose to eat the forbidden fruit, it opened doors for all evil. They chose to do what God had commanded them not to do. Next came the jealousy, hatred, and selfishness that was displayed through their son, Cain, when he killed his own brother. Today, sin is not at its highest level. The devil is still cunning in his evil ways. The ways of this world are growing increasingly evil every day.

Modern researchers have found that the church in America has little or no impact on the culture of the nation. Media has, by far, the most impact. As long as the church still exists and there are those being persecuted for being true followers of Christ, there is still some hope for the nation. We must run to receive the prize, not giving up or being overcome with evil, for there is still life in us.

CHAPTER 15
SPIRITUAL TRAINING

CONFRONTING SIN

I was one of the leaders of an interdenominational group at school, and the goal was to bring unity to the church of Christ and to reach out, with no limitations of religion. It was amazing to see how the church came together and began to trust one another in Rwanda after this terrible genocide.

Still, spiritually, our group was falling slowly. When the founders (visionaries) left after graduation, every year we received new people. I was left there to lead.

It seemed that I was speaking, but the response was quiet, and there was not much interest. I could feel a big fight in my spirit. Sometimes I felt it was spiritual warfare that leaders go through when they attempt to lead those under their authority. I stayed on my knees before the Lord and motivated more groups of intercessors to help me. Still a big group in the church had too much accusation against me, and they were agitating the whole church and other leaders. At the same time, I was voted to be one of the student representatives in the community, in charge of secretarial duties and security of the whole school of over a thousand students. My committee and I would walk around during the night to see what was going on.

Too many times I saw girls from the choir ministry out in the middle of the night with boys who never went to church—even with boys who were known at school as wild. The rules of the school said that students were not supposed to be out after 6:00 p.m. For me, it was too hard to tolerate deception in ministry, and I expelled them from the choir immediately.

One day I was invited to a meeting with the whole church, planned by this group of mostly girls and their boyfriends, and some of the leaders who were too interested in pleasing them. There were only two of us accused of talking too much about today's life, not only from the Bible. They said our teachings were not from God because we hurt people. They gave me three minutes to repent. I stood up slowly, trying to use the three minutes. I was angry with the people who chose me to lead, even though I was used to praying for them and loving them.

I said, "This is the end. I will never see you here again."

I meant that bad group, mentioning their names and what they do and the time they do it. Then I prayed that God would show the truth and judge us but also send them out of school, using the leadership of the school to catch them out sleeping with these boys.

The leaders of the school sent them away after two months. Some of them were afraid because many times I spoke things, and it happened so soon. They sent someone to apologize for them to me. God sometimes chooses the weaker followers to challenge the stronger ones.

One guy at school tried to corrupt me in a final test exam. The pagans were passing the answers on papers. He got the answers to the whole test. He cheated by giving it to me from under the table.

I said, "Hey, you must have me confused with someone else."

He looked at me. "Are you so stupid that you don't see that this is your answer, and this is free?"

Before I looked at it or passed it to the others, I crumpled it into a ball and threw it away. He got so angry, his eyes turned red, but he couldn't do anything. He had to wait until after the exam.

He came to me very soon after the math test. "You stupid Christian," he said. "You are an idiot, and you will never succeed in your life." I could tell he was tempted to punch me in the face.

I asked him, "Do you remember me before I got saved, when everyone respected me in the whole village?" I was referring to when I was a teacher of karate.

"Yes."

"Do you remember how bad I was, beating people for no reason? Jesus has changed me to be gentle and nice to everyone. Now you come to me calling me stupid. At the end of the year, we will see who is really the idiot."

Very near the end of that year, he was expelled from school because he was caught stealing school stuff. He had begun to smoke marijuana and other drugs and began to lose his mind. The next time I saw him, I was so sad—almost crying—because of the way he looked. From that time, I knew I had to control my anger and learn to forgive.

RELYING ON THE LORD

I remembered back when those discouraging things happened to me, I would go into the forest behind our school. I cried alone because non-Christians were telling me how I failed in many ways and they succeeded and how I looked stupid. I could see that was the way it appeared before the world, but still I had faith in the Lord.

I had a friend, Nitezeho, who was my encourager. Both of us shared some of the same problems, so we could help each other. One day the Congolese attacked his family in the neighboring country, Burundi. They killed his uncles, cousins, and aunts—all of them. He came to me to tell me that.

I was speechless, but he began to remind me that the earth is not our home. We prayed to God and read the Bible. Together we were still strong, even in loss. I have not met many strong men of faith like him. We became best friends.

In the way of success, there is failure. In spite of my friends and classmates making fun of me, even though I failed at school, I returned to that school to visit with an evangelism group.

When I went to school there, I had never spoken English. I had no one to teach me. It was amazing how I was the only one God used to interpret for some American preachers and some English teachers. They were so surprised because I was now able to communicate in both languages.

After the fellowship, one of the teachers came and asked me how I spoke English. I told her how God had gifted me in that. Praise God, she gave her life to Jesus right then.

Sometimes people make the mistake of thinking God uses them because of their strengths. Never forget that with God, all things are possible (Matthew 19:26). God only needs us to be available for Him. When God uses us in our weakness, all the glory is His. He doesn't need what we think we can offer to Him. God wants us to obey Him and walk in His ways. He tells us in Isaiah 49:23:

> Kings will be your foster fathers, and their queens your nursing mothers. They will bow down before you with their faces to the ground; they will lick the dust at your feet. Then you will know that I am the LORD; those who hope in Me will not be disappointed.

Paul warns us in 2 Timothy 3:7 not to be one of those who are "always learning but never able to acknowledge the truth." You must submit your life to the Lord and allow Him to teach you. There is no school or book that will ever replace the Bible and guidance of the Holy Spirit.

CHAPTER 16
TRUE REPENTANCE AND HEALING

EXPOSING DEEP WOUNDS

From the time I was saved, I focused my whole life on ministry and on reaching out to others. I never focused on my personal relationship and growth. I thought that God would take care of my business since I was taking care of his. When I joined Youth with a Mission, I learned how wrong I had been in my thinking.

In my Discipleship Training School, we had different teachings every week taught by different YWAM teachers. As I looked at our schedule of topics, I was confused. There were some teachings that I struggled with. Among them were "The Father Heart of God" and "Nature and Character of God." They seemed to be a waste of time, and I couldn't understand why they focused on such menial things in such a powerful school. I wasn't impressed by their schedule for the first three weeks because of overly simple lessons like those mentioned above.

They turned out not to be as simple as I thought. The teaching on "The Father Heart of God" was one of the most challenging to me. There were major questions in me that I had never addressed before, questions that many of us ask. Many of the other students seemed exasperated at first with all my questions, but then my questions became theirs as well.

"If God is a loving, almighty Father, I think he could have saved my family, but he didn't. Why?" That was my biggest question, for which I thought the teacher had no answer.

Without much talk, it seemed like the Holy Spirit was dealing with each one of us. Instead of impressive answers, the teachers used spiritual strategies. They gave us some Scriptures like "All have sinned and fall short of the glory of God" (Romans 3:23). That was not very impressive to me either.

"How about my little sister and brothers—were they sinners too?" I questioned again. It wasn't like I actually needed a logical answer, but I was trying to show God the wrong He had done in my life, as if He was the one who had killed my family. Maybe I just wanted to guilt Him into bringing them back, which was impossible. I really just needed to get healed from it.

Pastor Anastase was the teacher for that week on the "Father Heart of God." He was a nice tall dark-skinned guy, who seemed like he would be a very good father to his children. He asked each one of us to write one or more things down that had hurt us in the past—something very painful we wanted to bring to God.

For many years I was never able to tell anyone about my biggest failure of letting my little sister Christina go. She was killed right after I let her go, and I was much older than her.

Why didn't I keep her with me? Since I survived, she could have survived too, I thought. So I kept it a secret. For sure there was nothing I could have done to save her, but I hated the fact that I was alive and she was dead.

Even though it may sound so simple to write her name on paper, I couldn't bring myself to do it. My tears were not easily seen, but they seemed to fill all of me.

I was still lost in my struggle when Pastor Anastase told us to gather into groups outside of the classroom. I had not even been able to write her name down, but he then asked us to share our concerns in the group.

I chose one group that I thought I trusted. I remember saying it short and fast to avoid drawing any attention to myself. I knew that if I showed my sadness, my fellow Christian students would try to comfort me. Everyone mentioned their own struggle, and we went back into the classroom without any recognition of each other's hurts.

Pastor Anastase took our papers on which we had written our burdens and hurts outside, and we followed him. He laid them on the ground in front of a big cross, and then he asked one of us to set fire to the papers. It sounded simple, but as the fire burned, tears began to fall from every face.

My heart was so hardened. I wanted to explode into tears, but my pride still told me to calm down and be strong. He hugged us all and prayed for each of us. I couldn't wait to go back to class so that we could be released for lunch.

The next week we had another teacher who taught again about how God is a very loving Father, and He wants to heal us from our past. Our teacher was Elise. She was from Brazil and was always happy and smiling. She led us in worship with her guitar and spoke with so much life in her. When I looked around the classroom, there was joy overflowing.

My heart was troubled again about what I experienced the week before. *A loving Father again?* I thought my questions were already answered. I didn't know why I had to be troubled again. Why was I still so confused when everyone else seemed so happy? For the next hour, my body was in class, but my mind was being tortured far away.

After a while, I thought I couldn't help it anymore. I thought I was going to explode in front of everyone. I wrote on a piece of paper and gave it to one of our staff whom I trusted the most, "Brother, pray for me. I am troubled." Then I ran out the door without caution.

I fled to a maintenance closet, sat on the floor, and locked the door. It felt like just me and God there in that very dark room with the darkness that seemed to consume me. I had asked my teachers many questions that I didn't really expect them to be able to answer, but now it was time to be honest with God.

Was I going resist God and be the man who never cries, even alone in that closet? I had no more strength left to hold myself together, so I exploded before the God I had been told was my loving Father. My tears fell like a flood, and soon the closet was wet with them.

The man I had been pretending to be was completely broken. An hour passed and another began. I tried to reason through the situation and stop the feelings that shook me, but this time I had no control.

I had preached to people before about the love of God, but I had never really understood it. The same day that I had come to YWAM, I had preached with Youth for Christ, and many people got saved. I was all about doing God's business, but I never really let Him get into mine. My burden was still heavy; I had covered it with a lot of prayers and scriptures and then pretended I was okay.

Soon the class was over. Everyone had been praying for me. I had attempted to escape from this school many times before, and this time they thought I was gone. They looked for me everywhere. After my cries destroyed the wall I had built around myself, I fell asleep like a baby right there on the floor.

It was around ten in the morning when I locked myself that room, and I came out around 2:00 p.m.

Margaret, the school leader, waited for me in my room, praying that I would show up any time. She heard me opening the maintenance room door. She had the most caring heart of any woman I had met before. She was young, but acted with so much wisdom that you would think she was the oldest in this school. She got up from the bed, where she had buried her head in prayer and came to where I was.

With a look of surprise on her face, she asked, "Theo, are you okay? I thought you left."

Without an answer, I lay down on another bed and closed my eyes. I thought hard about how I would respond. She had so much spiritual authority she sometimes scared me.

She got up and walked slowly. Thinking that she had left, I opened my eyes to see her sitting next to me. She lovingly rubbed my arm, and I looked up to see her. Instead of her, though, I saw my mother. I knew that it was Margaret with me, but it was not her face that I saw. I don't remember her saying a single word, but I burst out into tears again.

She prayed with me for some time and then left, but I continued to cry for the next hour. I knew that God had not brought my mother back to life, but He had used His servant to show me His great love for me. If I could let go of myself, He would take good care of me as my own mother would.

Isaiah 54:11–17 says it this way:

> Afflicted city, lashed by storms and not comforted,
> I will rebuild you with stones of turquoise,
> your foundations with lapis lazuli.
>
> I will make your battlements of rubies,
> your gates of sparkling jewels,
> and all your walls of precious stones.
>
> All your children will be taught by the Lord,
>
> and great will be their peace.
> In righteousness you will be established:
>
> Tyranny will be far from you;
> you will have nothing to fear.
>
> Terror will be far removed;
> it will not come near you.
> If anyone does attack you, it will not be my doing;
> whoever attacks you will surrender to you.
>
> See, it is I who created the blacksmith

who fans the coals into flame
and forges a weapon fit for its work.
And it is I who have created the destroyer to wreak
havoc;
no weapon forged against you will prevail,

and you will refute every tongue that accuses you.
This is the heritage of the servants of the Lord,
and this is their vindication from me,"
declares the Lord.

I learned that while I questioned God and didn't believe He loved me or cared about me, He was only waiting for me to let Him heal me. But I was hiding in the Bible to cover my pain.

While we run away from Him, He is only waiting for us to change our minds or meet Him where we are. In His mercy, He protects us even when we are wrong, hoping we may look to Him and see His truth. But all we do is blame Him when things don't go as we think they should. We blame Him for our own failures and even wonder if He is alive or dead.

RECEIVING TRUE HEALING AND FREEDOM

After my DTS, I continued to work with the school, helping more broken people like me. I went with them on outreach, and many times students got sick due to our hard work and living conditions. It was on an outreach like this that I found myself exhausted, physically and spiritually. I was still carrying a burden in my heart.

I prayed, "Lord, I have tried my best. What I have left, undo that I may be free." There was a small voice inside of me urging me to repent publicly and free my soul from the guilt I had imposed on myself. The small voice kept whispering into my heart for some time. I couldn't see how I could do such a thing, to repent all my past to those who knew it.

I had a meeting with my pastor seeking council for my situation. I had asked him, "Do you think I need deliverance? It seems like everything I do fails."

The pastor looked at me with so much discernment and told me a parable he used many times. He explained that if there were no treasure in me, there would be no devil trying to steal it. It was when he told me to go and make sure I left nothing in my past unchecked that I had decided to take this action. It was that word of knowledge that he spoke to me that changed the course of my life.

Sometime before that, Margaret prayed for me and felt something was holding me back from reaching my blessings. She said that I seemed to be in spiritual prison. When I thought again about the small voice, I knew I had to act to free myself completely.

When I returned from outreach, I began to make a plan for my day of deliverance, inviting people to come and hear me repent. I had a hard time to find a name for that day, but it seemed so right to do it.

My friend and coworker, Geoffrey, had done the same thing, so I asked him to help me. Some people in YWAM knew what I was going to do because we lived together and they understood the power of repentance. I thought of inviting my whole family, YWAM family, church family, friends, and anyone else who knew me. The hard part was to tell them the reason for this occasion. I told no one, but I just invited them.

My brothers and sister were troubled about the invitation. Finally, they decided to come anyways to see what was going on with me. Vianney, my older brother, agreed to host it at his house. I began to invite people for a day of celebration and fellowship with family and friends. Many thought that maybe I would announce my engagement.

I prayed for money to buy food and drinks. I expected a lot of people, and I had not a penny in my pocket. The day got closer. Since I promised my brother to provide everything, he began to call me about it. I told him to wait as if I was busy. When it was one week before the scheduled event, I still had no money, so we moved it back another week. Five days before the rescheduled date, I was still praying for financing.

God's ways are truly higher than our ways. One of the DTS students from Canada, Nathan Smith, approached me with a bundle of money—seventy thousand Rwandan francs. The only thing he told me was, "Theo, I heard that you have some kind of special day, and I wanted to help you with something." It was the exact amount we needed.

As my coworkers had been praying for me, I approached them with the bundle of money in my hands. We were all amazed by God's surprising action through this young man's obedience to Him.

I organized the day, and my brother found ladies who surprised me with their professional cooking at the event. Everyone gathered to hear what I had to say. Around one hundred people were there, and no one had any idea what the day was all about, except for a few coworkers who helped me organize the whole thing.

After everyone ate and drank, my brother Vianney, the host, rose and welcomed everyone saying, "Today, we are here for a special day that Theo has prepared. But to be honest with you, unless he tells why we are here, none of us will know. So let us welcome him to tell us." Then he sat down.

I started by thanking my sister Mukashyaka, who took care of me when I was messed up after the war, when all my brothers had joined the RPF. I seemed unconscious back in those days, but she tried to help me. I handed her a small gift, then went on to my brother, Shyaka, who struggled to support me to go to school from the time I was a young boy until I was in high school. I thanked my aunt, who adopted me and helped me recover from my alcoholism, and my other brother, Ephrem, who came often to encourage me during and after the war and show me that we still had hope.

Finally, I got to my brother, Vianney, who had sent me one thousand francs when everyone else looked at my bad decisions and rejected me. "That small amount of money showed me the biggest love of Jesus in you," I told him.

Everyone was already touched just by that. My struggle with the devil began as I looked at this little girl of mine playing with her mom right in the front seat. I wondered what they all would think of me if I confessed my shameful actions. I struggled in my heart, wondering what to say next. Everybody sat in silence. I knew this was my chance to conquer my fear and break the chains that bound me. I knew the truth would set me free.

"Ladies and gentlemen, I have one more thing to confess: this young girl you see here is my own," I declared, as I motioned toward my little Sifa.

I paused, gathering my strength. Everyone who knew her mother and knew that she was my cousin sat with eyes wide open, waiting for my next words.

"And I want to ask for forgiveness from the great woman you see here, who struggled to raise this baby when I wasn't there. I have forsaken her and broke her heart. I want to make it clear that I was responsible and ask you all to forgive me. Even though I am a new person, I am still responsible for my past."

Having spoken my piece, I thanked everyone for coming. The burden that I had carried for so long fell off me immediately. I never felt as free and victorious as I did that day. I felt like a champion of my own life. I thank God for everything He had brought me through and for proving to me that He truly did care about my heart, my healing, and my freedom.

If we live a careless life, we are like an accident waiting to happen. Although in Christ we are forgiven of our sins, we still have to answer for the decisions we made, even those made in ignorance. The unchecked past may cause damages for our present and future. I feared the judgment of others if they knew of my mistakes, but I did not need their approval. I needed freedom for my soul. No matter what people may say, the sin inside of us is what goes with us wherever we go. That day, I exposed it to the light and ran.

To my surprise the Biguri (my seventh ancestry) family chief, M. Fidel, rose to conclude the meeting. I have never had anyone publicly speaking positively about me, but this time was beyond my expectations.

After a very long time searching for my way of redemption, I was given by this man the family blessing. My dad died before he could bless me or lead me into my manhood. I didn't know how to live on my own, but this time, God spoke to me through this man.

Our chief spoke, "First of all, I want to welcome you, Theo, into the family. Feel free and have no shame. In my whole life, I have never seen a man as bold as you are in this family. No one has ever been able to do as you did today." Then he turned to the elders of the family, who were seated together in the front. "None of us here, as old as we are, can speak the words you spoke in front of people. I want you to know that we will respect you and honor you. You are a very strong man."

Of course he couldn't say anything bad about someone in public, I thought. But then his speech continued to assure me God was really speaking through him.

"I give you your blessings. From now on, you shall be honored. None of your children will beg for bread. God shall bless the work of your hands."

When I heard these words, my heart jumped out of my chest. I remembered the words my pastor had spoken over me and I was amazed at the truth of God's promises.

REVEALING SECRET SINS

Sin begins in our mind, and then it becomes an action. When it is a continuous action that becomes comfortable, it becomes a character. Our character builds a culture, and culture will decide what can be acceptable, with no guilt attached. One action of compromise began with Eve, and now they are too numerous to count.

Thank God there is hope. Our hope resides solely in our salvation through Jesus Christ. We can run away from something outside of ourselves, but we can never run from what is within. Sin is a dangerous virus. You can run with it, sleep with it, or ignore it, but we all need the cure for it. The cure is only through the blood of Jesus Christ. It's very dangerous how we can simply make ourselves comfortable with our mess and act like nothing is wrong.

If you live in darkness, your eyes become accustomed to the darkness, and you begin to adjust to the darkness. This is a picture of how the world has lost the light, but it relies on a distorted sight of what is real. When the true light of Jesus is illuminated, we have the opportunity to know truly what we are talking about.

> Surely the arm of the Lord
> is not too short to save,
> nor his ear too dull to hear.
> But your iniquities have separated
> you from your God;
> your sins have hidden his face from you,
> so that he will not hear.
> For your hands are stained with blood,
> your fingers with guilt.
> Your lips have spoken falsely,
> and your tongue mutters wicked things.
> No one calls for justice;
> no one pleads a case with integrity.
> They rely on empty arguments, they utter lies;
> they conceive trouble and give birth to evil.
>
> —Isaiah59:1–4

So many times we think we are good because we go to church and Jesus died for our sin.

That is not what Christ died for. He died for us so that if we confess our sins, we may be forgiven. God wants to refine us.

He wants to continue His work in us. We live in an image of freedom, but we continue to live in the guilt of our past. But we can't just make Him our secret friend and expect Him to deal with our victims. This holds back our blessings in Christ. I think most people live under curses today—including sickness, depression, or failure—because they ignored this very important thing, which is the key to their own blessings.

We gather together, lay hands on those who are waiting for God to move, but not willing to do their part, and pray for hours or days, until nothing happens. We cry for them and begin to wonder if God wants to heal them or not. But the Scriptures tells us already that surely the arm of the Lord is not too short to save. I think our prayers are too short to release our answers because they are not complete. We all have to make our vow to the Lord and submit our history to the custody of our Savior.

The world is sick, and they need the Great Physician. Even the people of God carry a heaviness, and it can be caused by sin, wounds, or rejection. Sometimes it's caused by others. Sometimes it's self-inflicted. Sometimes it wasn't their fault, and they are true victims. There are many injustices that happen every day, even across these free countries, and very few wrongs are exposed to justice.

We often fail to show kindness to those we meet along the roads of life. We smile to one another, but are silently crying, hiding our wounds, going home alone, walking dead on the inside. Take your troubles and cares to the Lord in prayer, and as He promised, He will give you rest.

If you confess, there is only one to be embarrassed—Satan. Do not be afraid because it's life and death, and you have no choice but to make it right.

We are not called to fear man but to love him. Often our secret sins keep us from truly loving because the demeanor of our guilt gives us away. Freedom comes from confession. Trust is earned by confession. Our past is forgiven through confession.

Even after we are made right with God, we must make ourselves right with man if we want our love to be truly accepted.

Even if you have done things worthy of prison, know that a spiritual prison is worse than any physical one. There so many other things that are holding people, but remember Jesus's grace will not run out. He is still ready to forgive you.

A NEW NAME

From the time my daughter was born, there was a shadow on her life that kept her from true happiness. She was often violent with other children. It was because we shared the curses she was born into. Both of her parents struggled the same way.

Every time I visited her, she got angry with me for nothing. She even sometimes hid from me. She acted so violently and wanted somehow to defend herself from the spirit that attacked her. I knew something needed to change.

Confessing my sin publically was a simple action, but He did an amazing work out of my little step of obedience. After that day, I went to pick her up from my brother's house, where she stayed at the time. She stayed with me a few weeks at our mission base. This child surprised me with a new character, full of life and joy. She played with other kids and became friends with every person around. This time I knew that God had not only freed me but generations after me.

When she was born, my daughter was given two names. One of them reflected the shame that she was born into because of my actions. Since I had denied her, and people counseled her mother to abort her, she was given a name that meant, "God knows his own." This was not bad, but it still reflected the situation surrounding her birth. It was time to give her a new name that no longer carried the shame of her birth, but of her true worth. She did not need to carry the memory of all this rejection in her name.

I had to ask before I changed her name. She told me that she did not like the one name that I knew needed to be changed.

"Why?" I asked.

She didn't know why.

We chose a new name. I wrote three down and asked her to choose one. She chose Sifa, which means "praise." That name was perfect for her because I knew that we could praise God for my daughter. We loved each other so much, and she never wanted to leave me again.

RUNNING THE RACE OF FAITH

Finally I want to leave you with these thoughts from Scripture which sum up my life in so many ways:

> Brothers and sisters, I do not consider myself yet to have taken hold of it. But one thing I do: Forgetting what is behind and straining toward what is ahead, I press on toward the goal to win the prize for which God has called me heavenward in Christ Jesus.
>
> —Philippians 3:13–14

> The righteous cry out, and the LORD hears them; he delivers them from all their troubles. The LORD is close to the brokenhearted and saves those who are crushed in spirit.
>
> —Psalms 34:17–18

May you too be equipped to run with endurance the race set before you, with eyes fixed steadfastly on Jesus, the Author and Finisher of your faith. May His acquaintance with suffering give you comfort and courage to endure your own trials, and may you finish your race victorious in Him! (Hebrews 12:1–3).